Wild
MICHIGAN

Wild
MICHIGAN

By Jim DuFresne

NorthWord
PRESS, INC

BOX 1360, MINOCQUA, WISCONSIN 54548

© 1992 Jim DuFresne

Published by
NorthWord Press, Inc.
Box 1360, Minocqua, WI 54548

Designed by New Leaf Design,
Boulder Junction, Wisconsin

Edited by Greg Linder

For a free catalog describing NorthWord's line of nature books and gifts, call 1-800-336-5666.

ISBN: 1-55971-141-8

Library of Congress Cataloging-in-Publication Data

DuFresne, Jim.
    Wild Michigan / by Jim DuFresne.
        p. cm.
      1. Natural history—Michigan. 2. Natural history—Michigan—Pictorial works. I. Title.
QH105.M5D85 1992   92-9136
507.774—dc20   CIP

Printed and bound in Malaysia

Photography

Gerlach Nature Photography: pages 2, 8, 12, 14, 26, 38, 56, 57, 72-73, 76, 82-83, 90, 93, 94, 95, 96-97, 98-99, 100, 104, 105, 106-107, 112-113, 114

Rod Planck: pages 4-5, 6, 10, 13, 27, 28, 34, 36, 42, 46, 47, 48, 49, 54-55, 58, 60, 61, 62, 63, 74, 86, 92, 102, 106, 119, 126, 126-127, 128

Larry C. Tracy Jr.: pages 16, 23

David F. Wisse: pages 18-19, 20, 22, 24-25, 32-33, 40-41, 64-65

Daryl R. Beers: pages 11, 88-89

Natalie Miles: pages 30, 37

Reinhard Brucker: pages 116-117

Alan Charnley: pages 44, 53

Mary Slikkers: page 50

Mark S. Werner: pages 52, 84

Robert W. Baldwin: pages 66, 68, 69, 79, 80-81, 120, 125

Rosemary Van Houten: page 70

Dean Pennala: pages 77, 111

Carol Christensen: pages 78, 122

Jim DuFresne: pages 103, 108

Richard Stratman: page 124

PHOTO PAGE 2: The rugged Lake Superior shoreline in Pictured Rocks National Lakeshore. The park stretches for 42 miles along the south shore of the lake.

PHOTO THIS PAGE: Rippled sand in Sleeping Bear Dunes National Lakeshore, formed by the prevalent western winds off Lake Michigan.

PHOTO PAGE 6: The pitcher plant, a carnivorous plant that traps insects and thrives in the acid soil of bogs and wetlands.

To John Rusche,
Whose clear thoughts, sharp insights
and gentle pushes kept me on the path of my own choosing.
The mountains are as much yours as they are mine.
—j.d.

Contents

Introduction

I lit a match and it burst into flame. I touched a wad of paper with this short-lived torch, and small licks of fire climbed into a pyramid of kindling, eventually engulfing logs the size of my wrist.

Warmth, light, security. How many times in the woods has fire represented salvation at the end of a long hike? How often have I shaken off the cold, the wet, and the wind of the wilderness with a ritual that begins with a single match? Many times while researching this book, but not tonight.

Tonight I sit in my office, watching flames in a fireplace; watching them dance in the dead of winter. I'm sitting inside, clutching a mug of hot tea but looking outside at swirls of snow frosting the panes of my windows. I'm grateful for a roof over my head, but soon I'm reminiscing about journeys into the wilds of Michigan.

Remember that ten-mile trek across the Porcupine Mountains in a driving rain? Lord, what a hike.

How about the time a three-pound bass took my fly off the surface of Craig Lake?

And that cross-country portage on Isle Royale, when Lake Superior was whipping up waves too wicked for us to take on with our paddles.

And the loons. Who can forget the loons? I can hear them laugh now, in the dead of winter, because more often than not, wilderness is a place in the mind rather than some isolated point on the map.

You don't have to paddle the clear lakes of Sylvania Wilderness to appreciate the pristine setting. Just the notion that out there a place

LEFT: A dewy spider web in Alger County of Michigan's Upper Peninsula, which includes Pictured Rocks National Lakeshore.

exists where man is little more than a seasonal visitor is what's important. A place without roads, billboards, or society's jingles bombarding you from every direction is a sanctuary, even for those who will never set foot in it. The idea that a place somewhere hasn't been zoned, sold off, and posted with "No Trespassing" signs is in itself salvation from the bustle in which most of us live.

Michigan is blessed with many such places. Some are so large that it takes days to cross them on foot. Some are so small that their most isolated corners are but a 15-minute walk from your car.

There's Isle Royale, the island national park where, in 1964, I was enticed into the wilds by a father who was searching for northern pike in Lake Richie. Every decade since then, I've returned to the island as if I was on some pilgrimage to a Holy Land—and maybe I was.

There are the Porcupine Mountains, where I've struggled to the top of peaks for the sole purpose of basking in the view below.

There's the roar of the Menominee River, on whose whitewater I have ridden through Piers Gorge and the misty waterfalls that paint rainbows in the skies above Pictured Rocks.

In the Lower Peninsula, there are the wild and empty beaches of Big Sable Point and Negwegon State Park; the bugling elk of Pigeon River Country; and the island treks across Sleeping Bear Dunes' North Manitou Island.

Fifteen areas are described by words in this book, and many more are described by photographs. Still others are not described at all. Michigan is crowded with wondrous places.

The places you'll find in the book may not technically be considered wilderness, though many are defined as such by the government,

Above: Thunder Bay River in Alpena County. The river's headwaters are located in Montmorency County, and it empties into Lake Huron in downtown Alpena.

Right: Potawatomi Falls on the Black River in Gogebic County. In its final ten miles before emptying into Lake Superior, the Black River flows over seven waterfalls.

but they are wild one and all. They are places where I have wandered for years in the solitude and calm you find only when you're away from roads and cities. They are places that soothe the soul, rekindle the spirit, and strengthen the legs.

They are priceless places, threatened by the ever-increasing pressure of our wants and needs. Some of us desire the gas that lies beneath the surface, or the trees above. Others eye the rolling hills or ponds and see nothing but fairways and putting greens. Some of us want to build a cottage on the edge of the lake; others want to fly across the dunes in off-road vehicles.

I just want to keep them as they are. Once they're scarred by clear-cuts and condominiums, by washed-out roads and the roar of two-cycle engines, these precious few areas are lost—if not forever, at least for my lifetime. Worse yet, for the lifetimes of my children.

It would be a shame to grow up knowing that, no matter how far north you drive, the road will not end. Knowing that there's no lake without a motor on it, no stand of undisturbed, century-old oaks in the midst of which you might hear a leaf fall on a windless day.

It would be sad, indeed, if there was no wild Michigan free of fences where you could wander for miles, no place free of man where, on a cold winter night while watching a log turn to embers, you could wander in the back of your mind.

ABOVE: A fragrant white water lily on a pond in the Upper Peninsula's Luce County. The county includes the western half of Tahquamenon Falls State Park and the Two Hearted River, which was made famous by an Ernest Hemingway short story.

LEFT: Sunset on the Pictured Rocks. The cliffs change their colors hourly as the sun shifts its position.

13

Sleeping Bear Dunes

ooking to get away for a little adventure, two of us threw our backpacks together and headed for North Manitou Island, where we discovered that simply getting there was an adventure.

It began at the waterfront of Leland's Fishtown. On the weather-beaten docks, where commercial fishermen still mend their nets, we were joined by 50 more backpackers and a mountain of packs, tents, and other gear. We all bought our tickets, squeezed onto a small ferry, then waved goodbye to the Leelanau Peninsula and the rest of the mainland.

For the next hour, the vessel tossed and rolled among the Lake Michigan swells, making one passenger fall asleep and several more turn green. The rest of us were hanging on the railing or peering out of a porthole at a dark slice of island on the horizon. Excitement spread as the slice grew bigger, then abruptly turned to astonishment when we landed.

The boat stopped ten feet short of the beach. There was no dock, no National Park Service information center, no trail signs, not even a pit toilet. Just sand, surf, and a couple of park rangers waiting for the crew to extend a walkway from the bow to the beach.

We carefully tiptoed down the narrow gangplank and formed a line to unload the equipment.

Backpack after backpack was passed along to the shore. You could tell which ones had been thrown together at the last minute. Toothbrushes and sleeping bags spilled all over the place.

But the most amazing aspect of arriving at this wilderness island was watching the ferry leave. There's no turning back. You're stuck for three days in a place where travel is by foot, and a two-room suite is a tent with a vestibule.

This Robinson Crusoe-sensation prompted a little nervousness among us new arrivals, so the rangers jumped immediately into their orientation speech.

Pack out your trash. No washing in the lakes. No fires. Treat all water before drinking. And most important, spread out those campsites. Don't pitch 50 tents on the first scenic bluff along the trail.

"We don't want it KOA style, where tents are stacked on top of each other," added one ranger.

Wild Michigan? Definitely. North Manitou offers maybe the best wilderness experience in the Lower Peninsula. The 15,000-acre island is not only isolated from the mainland and for the most part undeveloped; it's preserved as part of the Sleeping Bear Dunes National Lakeshore.

The 71,000-acre national park is a hilly region that stretches on the mainland from Crystal Lake to the Good Harbor Bay, much of it fringed by the famous coastal sand dunes.

Chippewa Indian legend has it that a mother bear and her two cubs were driven into Lake Michigan by a raging forest fire. In their attempt to swim across, they were separated. The mother

LEFT: *Maple leaves at the height of fall colors in Alger County.*

15

eventually reached shore and, while waiting for her offspring, became Sleeping Bear, a solitary dune overlooking Lake Michigan. Her hapless cubs drowned, only to reappear as the Manitou Islands.

Scientists stand by a different explanation. They say the impressive dunes, some of which tower 460 feet above Lake Michigan, are the work of continental glaciers during the Ice Age. When the last glacier retreated 10,000 years ago, according to the scientific explanation, it left behind huge piles of sand in a setting ideal for the accumulation of dunes—a shoreline on the leeward side of Lake Michigan, where westerly winds created the shifting mountains of sand.

Without a doubt the most famous attraction in the park is the Dune Climb. Families from around the country come to struggle up the steep slope of a 130-foot dune, only to run back down after catching their breath at the top. At Pyramid Point, the perched dunes overlooking the lake are so steep and high that for years, when the

sport was more popular, this was a favorite launch site for hang gliding.

Sleeping Bear is much more than just dunes, however. It's an incredibly diverse landscape that ranges from the birch-lined Crystal River and a virgin stand of giant white cedar to miles of undeveloped beach along Good Harbor Bay. The seven-mile Pierce Stocking Scenic Drive, enjoyed by motorists and cyclists in the summer and Nordic skiers in the winter, swings past panoramic views of Glen Lake, Sleeping Bear Dune, and the endless blue horizon of Lake Michigan, ending in a quiet hardwood forest where a deer may be peeking from behind a maple tree. But to find the wildness in Sleeping Bear, you board a ferry in Fishtown.

Managed as a wilderness area, North Manitou Island has a ban on motors, off-road vehicles, mountain bikes, even wheeled carts that some might use to portage a boat to Lake Manitou in the center of the island. Although a few visitors arrive in private boats, the island offers no

LEFT: *A blowout dune area within Sleeping Bear Dunes National Lakeshore.*

OVERLEAF: *Sunset over Lake Michigan in P.J. Hoffmaster State Park. The 1043-acre park houses the Gillette Nature Center.*

protected anchorage, so the vast majority reach it by ferry. The ship runs only three times a week, forcing backpackers and others to stay at least two nights. But spending less time there would be a mistake.

North Manitou is almost eight miles long. It's four miles wide and laced with more than 22 miles of designated trail. Even more miles of unofficial trails and old logging roads wind among the impressive stands of maple and beech, along the shore of serene Lake Manitou, or through open dunes in the southern end of the island.

Along with dunes, great sunsets, and scenic places to pitch a tent are the visible signs of North Manitou's past. The 15-mile walk around the island presents faded barns, collapsed turn-of-the-century buildings, overgrown cemeteries, forgotten orchards, and other intriguing relics.

The heyday of island development was in the mid-1800s, when a lumbering community thrived here and loggers arrived to cut much of the original timber, even building a short railroad. Others followed to farm the land or plant apple and cherry orchards, while the U.S. Life-saving Service manned a station and lighthouse on Dimmicks Point to protect ships traveling through the wicked Manitou Passage.

By the 1930s, most of the island was under the single ownership of auto magnate William R. Angell, who turned it into a private preserve and released seven whitetail deer. In the absence of natural predators, the small herd exploded to more than 2,000 by the 1980s.

The National Park Service acquired control of North Manitou in 1984. Today in parts of the island, particularly in the rugged northwest corner, the forests are almost devoid of an understory because of heavy browsing by deer. The "grooming" gives the woods a park-like appearance. Wildlife often seen include chipmunks and raccoons, both of which are encountered too frequently to be natural.

Raccoons are especially common. Every summer there are stories about raccoons unzipping tents and stealing food bags and packs. For this reason, rangers urged us to hang food between two trees, as if we were in bear country. "They are bold. Not aggressive, but bold," said one ranger of the masked foragers.

The rangers maintain a station in what is referred to simply as "the Village," a cluster of buildings on the east side of the island. There are no stores or accommodations here, only an eight-site campground and a dock. At one time the ferries from Leland landed at the Village, but a sandbar eventually developed in front of the dock, forcing them to make on-beach landings in the southeast corner of the island.

Once on solid ground, most of the backpackers in our group beelined it from the landing site to the west side, where some of the most scenic campsites in the Lower Peninsula are found. One of them is called Swenson's Place, a clearing situated among the ruins of an old farm that includes an impressive if somewhat weather-beaten barn. All around are wild strawberries, raspberry patches, and panoramas of Lake Michigan.

Even closer to the landing beach, a mere two-mile walk, is Fredrickson Place. There are no buildings at this clearing, but you can camp on a grassy bluff high above the lakeshore and from your sleeping bag enjoy an incredible view of South Manitou Island and the dunes perched along the mainland.

North Manitou also offers the ultimate backpacking adventure in southern Michigan—skipping the trails altogether and following the island's shoreline. It's a 27-mile beach walk, and you encounter few if any people.

But my friend and I were smart backpackers. We skipped the beach and the west side and began hiking around the island on the east side. The easiest route, the one with the least climbing, involves walking the trails in a clockwise direction. By doing this, we ended up in the southwest corner of the island on our second day, with only a two-mile trek the next morning to catch the 11 a.m. boat.

And that was one ferry we didn't want to miss. It's a *looooong* three days if you do.

Big Sable Point

fter years of searching the Lake Michigan shoreline, I found what I never thought I would see.

While hiking from Manistee to Ludington, I approached the southwest corner of the Nordhouse Dunes Wilderness, and the single set of boot prints I had been casually following . . . disappeared. I walked another quarter-mile before the realization hit me—I was now on a stretch of beach without footprints. I walked on sand bearing no indication that anybody else had ever been here.

There were prints all around, but they were made by deer, seagulls, and the paws of some creature I couldn't identify. As far as people were concerned, I was it. I was the sole traveler on what has to be the most remote stretch of Lake Michigan shoreline.

Sand, surf, the dunes, and nothing more. No crowds and certainly no condominiums, no cars, no sea of coolers and beach blankets. Not even a footprint. Isolation is the most pleasant aspect of hiking the shoreline from Manistee County to Mason County, a 21-mile walk.

The other pleasure was stuffing my shirt and shoes into the pack and continuing in the soft sand without fear of stubbing a toe. When the temperature reached the mid-80s in the after-

noon, I took this beach-backpacking a step further and hiked through the gentle surf washing ashore. Finally I stopped for a refreshing dip, then laid in the sun, using my pack as backrest, on a beach that I could truly call my own.

I had two days of the most unusual trekking in the Lower Peninsula, past some of the state's most unique scenery, and it was made possible because a pair of parks contain and preserve Big Sable Point.

The first is Ludington State Park, a 5,200-acre unit in Mason County that includes 5.5 miles of Lake Michigan shoreline—the most of any park in the state. Ludington is a tourist haven. More than 700,000 people flock here annually to lay on the beach or fill up one of three campgrounds, where it's tough to get a site without an advance reservation. But that's all in the southern half.

The northern half of the park, almost 1,700 acres, is a state-designated Wilderness Natural Area, a trail-free, undeveloped area of open and forested dunes bordered on one side by a Great Lake and on the other by Hamlin Lake.

It's an area of small ponds and interdunal marshes that abound with waterfowl, shorebirds, and plant life in the spring, but may dry up completely by August.

It's hillsides or ravines of jack pine and hardwoods, slowly being buried by migrating dunes.

It's the open dunes that tower above the west shore of Hamlin Lake and look like a fortress of sand from the park's Island Trail.

LEFT: A ghost forest in the Nordhouse Dunes, which is a federally-designated wilderness area. The trees were killed by a migrating dune.

"It's an incredible area," said one park manager. "There are very few stretches of shoreline and dunes like this in the state. Every place else is built up."

Where the park's designated natural area ends, the Nordhouse Dunes begins—the only federally-designated wilderness in the Lower Peninsula. The dunes became part of the Michigan Wilderness Act of 1987 after much heated debate. Purists wondered how you could label an area that's only 3,450 acres—an area crisscrossed by old logging tracks and Forest Service roads—a wilderness. Oil companies bemoaned the lost chance to retrieve their precious mineral from beneath the surface, and others were angry that they would no longer be able to fly over the hills of sand on their off-road vehicles.

True wilderness or not, few will contest the notion that this niche of active dunes, wetlands, and rolling forests of hardwoods and conifers is unique in the Lower Peninsula. It's unusual even for this side of the state, which has long been revered by naturalists for the world's most extensive set of freshwater dunes.

Waterfowl, hawks, songbirds, and wildlife in general abound here, and on a beach hike your tracks mingle with theirs. Forget the bird book; instead, pack a guide to identifying prints. The shoreline of Nordhouse Dunes is a hodgepodge of tracks; from red fox, coyote, and raccoon to whitetail deer, which is the most common print in the sand—more common by far than footprints.

I began at the Magoon Creek Natural Area, a small township park located just south of Manistee, where I parked a car outside its gate and followed a foot trail to gain access to the shoreline. From here it was a trek of 3.5 miles to national forest land, reached by fording Cooper Creek, the first stream along the way.

The second stream that forced me to remove my boots was Porter Creek, and by scrambling through the ankle-deep water I entered the Lake Michigan Recreation Area. The national forest

LEFT: The open dunes found along Lake Michigan in the southern half of the Nordhouse Dunes Wilderness.

RIGHT: A red fox listens for an intruder. The species is common in both the Nordhouse Dunes and Ludington State Park.

campground is a popular facility where sites are spacious and well-separated. The campground is bordered on one side, naturally, by a towering, wooded dune. The beach, the woods, and the dunes are such an impressive combination that the recreation area was once called "one of the 20 best campgrounds in America" by a national magazine.

The campground is also a source of water. Fill up. The next source of safe water is eight miles away, because in-between is nothing but beach—the greatest stretch of undeveloped Lake Michigan shoreline, where you stand in the surf and all you can see is sand.

Inland, Nordhouse begins as a rolling terrain of well-forested and stabilized dunes. But eventually the trees give way to a tract of open dunes or to a light covering of beach grass. In some spots the dunes rise 140 feet above Lake Michigan. Many of them surround small parcels of vegetation and isolated woody patches of juniper and stunted jack pine.

These small stands of trees resemble islands in a sea of sand, and are some of the most unusual backcountry campsites in the state. The pines provide protection from wind, while their needles create a thin carpet over the loose

ground. My dome home was only a foredune away from the lake. At night, I sat on top of that hill and watched a clear blue sky give way to a spectacular sunset, and the last dying rays didn't melt into the shimmering Great Lake until well after 10 p.m.

End of day one on the beach.

On the second day, I passed only two landmarks in the beginning. The first was a small Nordhouse Wilderness sign marking the border between state and federal land, four miles beyond Porter Creek.

The second is quite large—the distinctive white and black tower of the lighthouse. Sharp eyes will usually pick it up more than a half-mile before reaching it. But I couldn't see through the morning fog, so I was a bit confounded when suddenly a gust of wind swirled the mist and then swept it away. There, not more than 300 yards distant, was Big Sable Point Lighthouse.

The light warns sailors of one of the most westerly points along this side of Lake Michigan. It took the sinking of the barge *Neptune*, an incident in which 37 died off the Point in 1848, to stir the federal government into building the light station. President James Buchanan approved the funds in 1858, but actual construction

ABOVE: Lake Michigan shoreline bordering the Nordhouse Dunes. Combined, the Dunes and Ludington State Park preserve more than seven miles of undeveloped lakeshore, including Big Sable Point.

didn't begin until President Andrew Johnson ordered it in 1866.

On Nov. 1, 1867, the light was illuminated by Burr Caswell, the first white settler in Mason County and the first lighthouse keeper. Big Sable Point used a Fresnel lens that was shipped from Paris and cost more than $1,000. The signal was a fixed white beam that burned 179 gallons of "refined lard wick oil" during the shipping season from April to November, the only time it was operated. In 1908 the federal government installed Michigan's only two-tone, air-diaphone fog signal here and operated it on compressed air. By 1968 the lighthouse was fully automated, and the fog signal was discontinued two years later.

The reason for the lighthouse is the Point, which worried seamen but is a delight to hikers who love to beachcomb. This shoreline catches everything the winds and currents sweep across the Great Lake, from the delicate skeleton of a salmon and the root system of an entire tree to a milk bottle from Green Bay, the colorful bobbers of fishermen, and somebody's lost lone tennis shoe.

The lighthouse also marks the beginning of the developed portion of the state park, and departure from the remoteness of the dunes. Within two miles you'll encounter a bathhouse near the mouth of the Big Sable River, an army of beachgoers if it's summer, and the sound of traffic on M-116, which borders the shoreline here. Hike a few more miles and you end up in downtown Ludington.

But there is something satisfying about traveling from one city to the other on foot— knowing that if you follow the line between the water and the sand, you will never get lost. And in spending a quiet night on a dune watching the moon rise out of the lake, you might even find yourself.

ABOVE: Frosted grasses in an Alger County meadow. Early morning frost can be a common occurrence in the Upper Peninsula, beginning as early as mid-August.

RIGHT: A northern hawk-owl surveys the winter landscape of the Upper Peninsula. The medium-sized, hawk-like owl often perches at the tips of trees, but it sits in a less erect posture than other owls.

Lake Michigan State Parks

Why wait until July?

As popular as hiking is, and as many foot trails as Michigan has, some people still think a walk in the woods is something done in summer. If there aren't bugs in the air and leaves on the trees that obscure the view from hilltops, it's not the season for hiking.

Excuse us, but my five-year-old son and I disagree. We'll trade you a July or an August hike for an April or a May one anytime.

There may be a foot of snow somewhere in the Upper Peninsula, but in southern Michigan people begin lacing up their hiking boots in April, and Michael and I were among them when we arrived at Saugatuck Dunes State Park.

Sure, it was nippy. So we pulled our wool hats down past our ears, stuffed our hands deep in our pockets, and rejoiced in what we perceive as perfect hiking conditions. The sun was out, the sky was blue, the snow was gone, and the state park was virtually empty.

State parks are scattered throughout Michigan, from the shores of Lake Erie (Sterling State Park) to the tip of the Keweenaw Peninsula in Copper Harbor (Fort Wilkins State Park). But the most unique ones are those along Lake Michigan that preserve and showcase the greatest set of freshwater dunes in the world.

LEFT: A migrating dune spills into the picnic area of Warren Dunes State Park, at the southeast corner of Lake Michigan.

However, the rugged terrain of the dunes, the long stretches of sandy beach, and the spectacular sunsets also make these parks the most popular in Michigan.

By far.

Holland State Park is traditionally the most crowded, drawing 1.5 million visitors a year. Grand Haven State Park attracts 1.3 million; a campsite there is so much in demand that a lottery is held on the first working day of January, and reservation requests are picked from a hat. The beach at Warren Dunes has a parking lot with room for more than 2,000 cars, yet on many summer weekends the staff is forced to close the gate and turn away afternoon arrivals. There's simply no place to park their vehicles.

Wild Michigan? Not in July.

My son and I avoid those parks in summer like a plague of black flies, arriving instead during the off-season. Warren Dunes is spectacular in October. The 1,507-acre park, the first unit along Lake Michigan, features 2.5 miles of sandy shoreline, and a dedicated natural area in its northern half where you can hike through a series of wooded and open dunes.

Its most noted feature, however, is Tower Hill, the tallest dune in the park at 240 feet. During the mid-1970s, the hill became a haven for hang gliders. On a windy weekend back then, it was not unusual to see almost 100 gliders on its slope and 20 in the air at one time. The park staff, overwhelmed by the number of accidents

occurring among unqualified flyers, instituted stricter regulations and a permit system. But even today on most September and October weekends, you can watch a handful of these colorful adventurers soaring off Tower Hill and riding the smooth Lake Michigan winds to the soft and forgiving beach below.

To the north is Grand Mere State Park, a unit of almost 1,000 acres with such unique land formations and flora that it has been designated a National Natural Landmark. The glaciers that scooped out the Great Lakes 10,000 years ago also carved a number of smaller depressions along the western edge of the state, and these evolved into interdunal lakes. At one time Grand Mere contained five such lakes, protected by a line of wind-blown dunes. Today the park has only three, and the area is studied as a textbook example of aquatic succession. You can begin at North Lake and notice how each lake is progressively disappearing as open water turns to marsh and eventually woodland. The last two lakes in the chain are no longer lakes.

The dunes not only protect the lakes, but produce an unusually cool environment that results in habitats and plants found nowhere else in southern Michigan. Hemlock and white pine give the park a touch of the boreal forest normally seen only in northern Michigan, while the profusion of wildflowers includes the rare starflower.

Perhaps the best place to study sand dunes is P.J. Hoffmaster State Park, a 1,043-acre unit just south of Muskegon. A ten-mile network of trails loops through the park and allows visitors to view the plant succession that the dunes display so well, from the barren sand of the beach along Lake Michigan to the dune grass and other pioneering plants to the back dunes forested in white pines and black oaks. All of this is clearly explained at the Gillette Nature Center, the park's interpretive center, which is literally overshadowed by a huge, wind-blown dune viewed through a glass wall on the west side of the lobby.

You can also see it from the Dune Climb. Located near the nature center is a winding stairway that climbs 165 steps to a spot above the trees at the crest of a dune. From the observation deck 190 feet above Lake Michigan, your efforts are rewarded with a panorama of Lake Michigan and miles of its shoreline. But most impressive are the dunes you see in almost every direction. Without question, you're in dune country.

Then there's Silver Lake State Park in Oceana County. The park contains 2,800 acres, and 1,800 of them are located in a mile-wide strip of backcountry between Silver Lake and Lake Michigan. Here lie some of the barest dunes found anywhere in the state. Many of them are steep hills without so much as a blade of beach grass, and are slowly shifting east, giving the area a Sahara Desert sort of appearance.

But Michael and I like Saugatuck State Park in Allegan County. There's no campground at Saugatuck, nor any facilities beyond vault toilets, a hand pump for water, and picnic tables. The park does feature two miles of Lake Michigan shoreline, but there's no easy way to reach this stretch. You can't drive to the beach—not yet, anyhow—and the shortest trail to the lake is a one-mile walk from the parking lot. That's why we like it.

Arrive at this foot-traffic-only park in the middle of the week in April, and it's yours. All 844 acres, all 14 miles of trails, all two miles of glorious beach. Maybe it's too cold to go swimming, but we can sit on a high sandy bluff and enjoy our lunch with a view that doesn't include a single beach towel or lawn chair.

That's just not possible in July.

We departed the parking area, entered the woods through the trailhead to the south, and immediately skirted the Michigan Dunes Correction Facility. That's the bizarre aspect of this park—having to hike around the barbed wire fence of a jail. When prison officials made an announcement over the public address system, Michael and I froze in our steps, half-expecting a handful of armed guards to jump out from behind the trees. They didn't, so we hurried along the footpath to the marked junction of the

Livingston Trail, a half-mile, one-way path that extends from the park's southern loop to Lake Michigan.

The park was a political trade-off after the St. Augustinian Seminary, faced with a dwindling number of students and growing debts, sold the land and its 30-year-old school building to the state in 1977. When citizens in nearby Holland and Saugatuck heard rumors that the area would host a 400-bed correctional facility, they protested loudly and organized opposition to the plan. Despite their overwhelming protest, crime won out. But to calm citizens, Governor William Milliken declared that all but 50 acres of the tract would become Michigan's newest state park.

So we passed barbed wire and bullhorns on our way to sand dunes and shoreline.

Park maps label the Livingston Trail as "most difficult," but that's for skiers in the winter, who may find themselves flying uncontrollably downhill. In April this trail was an easy trek, beginning in a wooded hollow formed by a pair of towering dunes. We actually skirted the side of the dune to the south, and through the leafless trees we could see everywhere. At the crest of a dune to the north, a pair of deer appeared.

Eventually the trail climbed over the dune and dropped into a second wooded ravine, this time descending right to the bottom before climbing again. We emerged at the edge of a sandy bluff overlooking Lake Michigan, where we pulled out sandwiches and a thermos of hot chocolate from my day pack.

The food and warm drink were strictly secondary to the view. The spring sun had already opened up the first stretches of sandy beach, but it had a ways to go along the water's edge, where the shore ice was still piled high. Further out, we saw a spattering of small white icebergs and then the blue horizon of Lake Michigan. To the north, the scene was crowned by the distinctive red of the Holland Lighthouse.

Light brown, brilliant white, deep blue, and a touch of red. It was quite a panorama. And you'll see it only if you go hiking in early spring.

31

Manistee National Forest

Long after the summer season had passed, but before the leaves began to drop, I spent a day hiking the North Country Trail in the Manistee National Forest. The path was mine, I thought, so I let my legs walk and my mind wander amidst the brilliant autumn colors, the crisp October air, the silence that had settled among the oaks and maples.

At one point I looked casually down the path, only to face the most frightening encounter with wildlife I've ever experienced. I was much calmer when a humpback whale surfaced 20 yards from my kayak in Alaska; dealing with a 400-pound black bear in northern Minnesota was nothing compared to what was approaching me now.

Strolling along the trail—*my* trail—with its nose to the ground and not a worry on its mind, was a skunk, striped tail and all. I stopped, but he was oblivious to my presence. The thought of being attacked by his defensive gland and then having to hike four miles back to the car had my heart pounding. It was obvious the path was not wide enough for both of us, so I gambled and did something reckless.

I cleared my throat. The skunk stopped, looked up for the first time, and for a split second, a delicate stand-off prevailed on the North Country Trail. Man and animal faced each other,

ten yards apart in the middle of the woods; one was as terrified as the other, and neither was quite sure what to do.

We both made a conscious choice. I departed the trail in one direction, and the skunk, luckily, took the other. We scurried through trees, rustling the dried ferns at a panicked pace before returning to the path. We could hear each other, but not once did I look back at my brief acquaintance, and I was another mile down the trail before my heart stopped pounding.

Before the day was over, I covered 22 miles on foot. I crossed a few forest roads, but saw not one house. I encountered a dozen deer, two flocks of wild turkeys, and salmon spawning up the Manistee River, but not a single person. I climbed steep ridges and hills, enjoyed panoramas from the clearings on top, and even had a little hair-raising adventure. Not once did I leave the North Country Trail. At the end I was amazed that such ruggedness, such solitude, and such wooded beauty could be found so close to home.

. . . .

The Manistee National Forest was established in 1938, 23 years after the Department of Agriculture formed the U.S. Forest Service to manage a growing string of national forests across the country. Although the original forest was eventually reorganized as part of the Huron-Manistee National Forest, that's a distinction

LEFT: *Maidenhair fern is a common ground cover in the sandy soil of the Manistee National Forest.*

significant only to administrators. Hikers, campers, and anglers still view it as the Manistee National Forest, a patchwork of public lands on the west side of the Lower Peninsula that extends from Hodenpyl Dam Pond and Mesick in the north to almost Muskegon in the south, and from Lake Michigan in the west to Cadillac in the east.

Within this area you'll find 18 developed campgrounds with more than 400 sites, miles of foot trails, and the Nordhouse Dunes, the only federally-designated wilderness in the Lower Peninsula. The forest is a land of rivers with excellent canoeing in the Pine, White, and Big and Little Manistee rivers, and noted fishing in the Muskegon River.

Then there's the Pere Marquette.

Seventy miles north of Grand Rapids, the Pere Marquette is the only free-flowing river system in the Lower Peninsula, its waters not impounded by dams or other barriers. The river is so crystal-clear, and its natural beauty is prized by so many, that in 1978 the U.S. Congress designated 66 of its miles—from the junction of the Middle and Little South Branches near Baldwin to U.S. 31 at Ludington—as Michigan's first National Scenic River.

In the west portion of the national forest is the Lake Michigan Recreation Area, where two platforms situated on the top of towering dunes provide sweeping panoramas of the shoreline along the Great Lake.

In the heart of it is the Bowman Lake Foot Travel Area, whose rolling, glaciated hills and pristine lake are set aside strictly for non-motorized use.

And to the south near White Cloud, the forest includes Loda Lake Wildflower Sanctuary, a preserve for wildflowers and other protected plants.

Although spread out and pieced together, the Manistee National Forest does have one connecting thread—the North Country Trail. It enters the forest near Hodenpyl Dam, crosses all those rivers at one point or another, winds past many of the campgrounds, cuts through the foot travel area, swings near the wildflower sanctuary, and touches the shores of dozens of lakes. Finally it ends where the national forest ends, at the Muskegon River near Newaygo, waiting for additional segments to be built to complete its march toward Ohio.

It's one amazing foot trail. When completed, this route will extend 3,246 miles, from the Lewis and Clark National Historic Trail at North

Dakota's Lake Sakakawea to Crown Point overlooking Lake Champlain in New York's wild Adirondack State Park. In between, it will traverse a wide variety of scenic, natural, and historic areas in seven northern states, becoming the longest component of the nation's only transcontinental trail.

The idea for such a trail first popped up in 1965, as part of the U.S. Forest Service's "Nationwide System of Trails Study." Ten years later, the Department of the Interior recommended that Congress enact legislation authorizing the North Country Trail. In March of 1980, Congress did, directing the National Park Service to administer the trail's construction in cooperation with federal, state, and local agencies. The North Country Trail Association was quickly formed to handle the responsibility of building what is officially called the North Country National Scenic Trail. Hikers affectionately shorten it to "NCT."

More than 1,400 miles of the trail have since been built and are being used today. Unlike the Appalachian Trail and the Pacific Crest—national trails that follow the crest of mountain ranges—the North Country Trail journeys through a variety of environments and terrain. It will include the Adirondack Mountains in New York; the hardwood forests of the Allegheny Plateau in western Pennsylvania; the simple beauty of rural Ohio; the glacier-carved lakes of Minnesota; and the endless plains of North Dakota.

But clearly the crowning jewel of what will become the longest continuous trail in the country is the portion within Michigan. The state will contain 875 miles of the North Country Trail—more than any other. The segment in the Ottawa National Forest and the Porcupine Mountains Wilderness State Park in the western half of the Upper Peninsula is considered the wildest and most remote stretch. The 200-mile segment from Munising to St. Ignace is the longest completed section to date, and it's on this portion that hikers pass such natural treasures as Tahquamenon Falls, Pictured Rocks, and Grand Sable Dunes.

Eventually the trail crosses the Mackinac Bridge to the Lower Peninsula and heads south for Ohio, passing through Wilderness State Park, the Jordan Valley, and merging with the Shore-To-Shore Riding and Hiking Trail south of Traverse City. But the longest portion that has been cut and posted south of the Straits of Mackinac—more than 100 miles—is the trail that bisects the Manistee National Forest.

It seems only proper, then, that in the middle of the Manistee National Forest, less than a half-mile from the trail but seemingly in the middle of nowhere, is a 100-year-old schoolhouse whose importance is missed by most who travel here. A statement of its significance is posted right above the front porch. You're notified that if you head *this* way, you'll reach North Dakota and the western end of the trail in 1,633 miles. If, on the other hand, you head *that* way, you'll arrive at New York in 1,603 miles.

Because the schoolhouse lies practically on the halfway point of the trail, Birch Grove Township donated the historical building to the North Country Trail Association in 1980. Today, most of the building is used as a youth hostel, while its six-foot by six-foot entry, complete with a desk, a telephone answering machine, one file cabinet, and a sagging cot, serves as headquarters of the association responsible for building a 3,200-mile-long trail. Born of small beginnings, lots of volunteers, and big dreams.

The first NCT section built in Manistee National Forest was an 11-mile stretch from near Baldwin south to Nichols Lake National Forest Campground. But the most spectacular stretch, providing access to one of the most remote areas in the Lower Peninsula, is the 20-mile trek from Hodenpyl Dam Pond along the Manistee River until you cross it at High Bridge. Few trails in the Lower Peninsula can match the natural beauty, the number of scenic vistas passed, or the rugged terrain that this section of the North Country Trail reveals.

· · · · · · · ·

I began at first light, the only car at the small trailhead parking lot. Within a half-mile I emerged from the pines to an overlook of the Manistee River, with the man-made Hodenpyl Dam Pond off in the distance and everything bathed in the soft glow of a rising sun. Two miles later I was deep in the woods, climbing in and out of one ravine after another. During the most intriguing part of the hike, I made a mile-long ascent along the ridge bordering the river valley, descending then into ravines before climbing out and crossing over to the next slope.

The ascent really didn't end until I reached a faded wooden sign that proclaimed "Red Hill Overlook." The trees open up at the 1,105-foot high point, so I leaned against one, caught my breath, and studied miles of landscape to the southeast while the outlines of several steep ridges lay at my feet, in the direction I had to go.

What a trail! My heart was pounding again. And this time, there wasn't a skunk in sight.

LEFT: *Heal-all wildflowers. Their Latin name is* Prunella vulgaris, *but the delicate and colorful blossoms are anything but vulgar.*

OVERLEAF: *A sugar maple begins its transformation to autumn red. In southern Michigan, fall colors peak from mid to late October.*

Huron National Forest

7he brochure wasn't kidding.

The two skiers picked it up at the U.S. Forest Service office in Harrisville and read it before reaching the Hoist Lakes area of the Huron National Forest. The brochure described Hoist Lakes as "designed with the more experienced skier in mind. Longer loops and steeper hills offer an exciting challenge."

The challenge presented itself 30 minutes into the trip. Just after the skiers skirted the shores of frozen Byron Lake, the trail began a steep ascent. They tried striding up, but the angle was so sharp that they quickly switched to a herringbone. At one point, while taking a well-deserved break, they even considered removing their skis.

When they reached the top, their thighs were aching, their hearts were racing, and the vapor pouring out of their jackets was steaming up their glasses. But the long haul was worth it. They had reached a high point of 1,140 feet and, from a clearing among the trees, the skiers discovered a 180-degree panorama of the rugged terrain leading southwest to the Au Sable River, all of it pristine in winter's white.

The excitement followed the challenge. The trail departed on the backside of the hill, making a rapid descent to a frozen pond. For more than a

Left: A small stream flows through an evergreen swamp in the Huron National Forest.

half-mile of sharp turns and fast skiing, the two backcountry travelers crouched low in their skis and grimaced only when the cold wind whipping past turned their cheeks pink. Soon, icicles dangled from one skier's mustache.

By the time the skiers finished the eight-mile loop, stopping only to have lunch on another frozen lake, they were convinced that this slice of the Huron National Forest offers the best backcountry skiing opportunities in the Lower Peninsula.

But Hoist Lakes is far more than just a cross-country ski area. It's part of the great forest named Huron.

. . . .

The Huron is half of the Huron-Manistee National Forest, and the land is just that—forest controlled by a federal agency. The land is managed under a "multiple use" concept, so timber and other renewable resources are harvested, hunting and trapping are allowed, and facilities for recreational activities such as camping, hiking, and boating are provided.

Yet the main purpose of the National Forest System has not changed through its first century, and that purpose is conservation, or, as one ranger put it, "caring for the land and serving the people."

The movement aimed at preserving forests began in the late 1800s, when logging companies were harvesting trees to meet the timber needs

ABOVE: The standing water of a Lower Peninsula swamp. The wetland is more than a haven for breeding mosquitoes. The dead trees provide excellent habitat for nesting waterfowl, and trunk cavities serve as nests for other bird species.

of a growing nation and leaving behind little more than a wasteland of stumps. In the process, watersheds were destroyed; soil erosion was rampant; and entire species of animals were obliterated. Nowhere was this more evident than along Michigan's Au Sable River.

Many Americans at the time believed that the country's timber resources were unlimited; others justified the abuse of land as a necessary consequence of development. But by the 1890s a growing number of conservation leaders, including Theodore Roosevelt, advocated public ownership of land and management of that land for the common good over the long term.

On March 3, 1891, Congress passed the Forest Reserve Act, which empowered the president to set aside national forests. By the end of that

month, President Benjamin Harrison created Yellowstone Park Timber Land Reserve.

Despite vehement opposition, many of the national forests were established by 1908; there are now 156 national forests in the country, ranging from the Caribbean National Forest of Puerto Rico to the Tongass National Forest in southeast Alaska, a 16-million-acre preserve bigger than the state of Connecticut. The 191-million-acre National Forest System is spread from Florida to Washington. And Michigan is blessed with a good slice in the Huron-Manistee, Hiawatha, and Ottawa national forests.

The Huron can be traced back to 1909, when a presidential proclamation created a national forest from abandoned farms and lumbered wastelands around the heavily logged areas of the Au Sable River. It was later named Huron National Forest, and in 1938 large tracts on the west side of the state were added. The million acres that resulted were eventually combined and administered as single unit, the Huron-Manistee. But most people—and many of the Forest Service brochures—still view the units separately.

And they are separate. The Huron harbors a national scenic river in the Au Sable; a national forest scenic byway in River Road; and miles of trails for hikers, skiers, and snowmobilers. The latter mileage includes a good portion of the Shore-to-Shore Hiking-Riding Trail, a 200-mile pathway that cuts across the Lower Peninsula from Empire on Lake Michigan to Tawas City on Lake Huron. The forest also contains 12 developed campgrounds, but its most noted attraction is Lumbermen's Monument, overlooking the Au Sable River.

The impressive bronze statue of three loggers was erected in 1931, and the lumbermen are now surrounded by the same kinds of trees their living counterparts were cutting down a century ago. Even more impressive is a nearby interpretive area with a museum and hands-on exhibits. The area puts the logger into proper perspective. Viewed by many today as a colorful, Paul-Bunyan-like character who wore Mackinaw shirts and ate fry cakes for breakfast, the logger was, in reality, cheap labor. In the middle of winter, he made $2 for 12 hours of pulling a saw while cold water sloshed in his boots. It's little wonder that by the time most loggers turned 35 years old, they were too worn out or too sick to continue in their trade.

The forest campgrounds are nice and the interpretive area is revealing, but visitors needed more. In the late 1970s, the U.S. Forest Service began setting up foot travel areas throughout national forests, to provide a quiet sanctuary from the noise and rumble of today's motorized society.

In the Huron National Forest there is Reid Lake, a 3,000-acre area surrounding a small lake with six miles of trails winding through the gently rolling terrain. And there's Wakeley Lake Foot Travel Area, a walk-in fishing area renowned for its trophy bluegill and bass.

But the largest and thus the quietest area is Hoist Lakes, located 22 miles west of Harrisville. Encompassing 10,600 acres, the foot travel area is composed of ridges and hills, some topping off at 1,200 feet, along with seven small lakes. That's enough woods and hills for a legitimate backpacking trip. You can sneak off here for days at a time.

Many people enjoy hiking in to some of the most scenic backcountry campsites in the Lower Peninsula, while anglers who like to cast into a lake they can call their own—even if only for one afternoon—have discovered the walk-in fishing opportunities. The only catch to all this adventure is that you have to reach it on foot, whether by skis, snowshoes, or that well-worn pair of hiking boots. Cars, all-terrain vehicles, and even mountain bikes are banned from Hoist Lakes. It's simply a sanctuary for the feet, and for those searching out a quiet spot in the woods.

The avenue of travel is a 20-mile network of trails that forms two basic loops, each with its own trailhead. The West Loop is a 7.8-mile hike from its trailhead on De Jarlais Road. It passes three lakes and climbs over the 1,140-foot ridge where the two skiers experienced one of the most scenic vistas on the east side of the state.

Less than two miles from the trail's beginning, you emerge at the north end of Byron Lake, the second largest in the area. Carry in a canoe if you can, or a belly boat (a covered innertube) if you can't, and spend an afternoon tossing spinners for smallmouth bass. Better yet, carry in a tent and set up camp at one of the lake's three backcountry campsites. They offer little more than a tent pad, a fire ring, a log bench some backpacker made long ago, and a stairway down to the lake. But they're situated on the edge of a bluff surrounding the lake, and you awaken to a view of Byron Lake and the forested ridges that surround it. Not a bad way to start a morning.

The East Loop is an 11-mile trek with a trailhead off M-65. Much of the northern half winds through clear-cuts that most hikers and skiers would rather avoid. The Forest Service has discontinued its policy of allowing logging in foot travel areas, but it's a rather dismal experience to enter a field of stumps, brush piles, and matchstick sapling that will not be a forest in your lifetime.

ABOVE: A nesting Canada goose with young. The species is the most widespread goose in North America, and thousands migrate annually through Michigan.

LEFT: Fringed polygala in full bloom.

But the stretch of the trail from the east parking lot south to Hoist Lakes is an enjoyable journey past marshes and ponds and over ridges with extensive views of their own. More scenic backcountry campsites are situated on a bluff overlooking South Hoist Lake, which is stocked annually with rainbow trout, while a few steps away is North Hoist Lake, where I once sat for hours watching a beaver tend to its lodge.

It's possible to observe a variety of wildlife from either loop, especially near the many ponds, marshes, and small lakes that break up the forest. The most famous residents of the area are the least-encountered ones—the black bears. Red foxes, minks, and coyotes are also found here, but backcountry travelers are more likely to encounter flocks of wild turkey, ruffed grouse,

white-tailed deer, porcupines, and a variety of birds and waterfowl.

You can camp anywhere in foot travel areas, as long as you're not within 200 feet of an open body of water or a trail. Good off-trail spots for either summer or winter camping abound in the Hoist Lakes area, but why go any farther than those scenic campsites?

The nicest aspect of this backcountry area is not the views from above, the rugged terrain, or the lakes stocked with trout. The true beauty of Hoist Lakes lies in the lack of crowds and the availability of an open campsite—even on the weekend.

And the only price you pay is a little boot leather.

ABOVE: A wild iris emerges from a stand of sensitive fern near Lake Huron. The wildflower is widely distributed throughout Michigan.

RIGHT: A spring pond in Jonathon's Woods. The 144-acre preserve in Lapeer County features heavily forested hills, steep ravines, bogs, and ponds that support more than 300 species of plants.

Pigeon River Country

After moving to Michigan in May, Susan drove north one weekend to see the one thing in the woods she never would have seen in New Hampshire—an elk. She joined a nature center's annual fall excursion to the Pigeon River Country State Forest, and with ten others spent a Friday evening driving along rutted two-track roads and looking at empty fields.

It was almost dusk when the group decided to stop once more at the most logical of all places, a field posted with an "Elk Viewing" sign. "We joked about it later," she said. "It's as if the state could put up a viewing area sign and say, 'Okay people, go here. Elk come here, and we'll get you together.'"

Not quite together, but close. This particular viewing area was a traditional gathering spot for the herd, enhanced even more by biologists who had planted rye, clover, and other crops to attract the large herbivores. The state forest staff then cleared out a parking area with a good view of the field and surrounding woods, and finally erected a sign along the road.

It worked. As dusk turned to dark, Susan saw her elk—actually a herd of eight, intermingled with more than a dozen whitetail deer. "It was absolutely amazing," she recalled. "They're such big animals."

LEFT: The Pigeon River flows through a grassy meadow. The river begins east of Gaylord and flows north into Mullett Lake.

They are. An average adult bull weighs 750 pounds, and several have tipped the scales at more than 900 pounds. The rack on many male adults is a yard wide. Adult cows weighs 525 pounds, and even a six-month-old calf is a 300-pound animal. They're big, they're impressive, and you'll find nothing like them in New Hampshire. Or Ohio or Indiana or Illinois or, for that matter, anywhere east of the Mississippi River—the reason Susan and thousands of others come to Michigan every fall from across the state and the Midwest.

Today the state's elk herd is about 1,100 strong, roaming a 1,000-square-mile range that includes portions of Cheboygan, Otsego, Montmorency, Emmet and Alpena counties. Although stray elk have been seen as far south as the high school football field in Mio, the heart of their range is the 98,000-acre Pigeon River Country State Forest, an area whose history with man is as bumpy as the pothole-filled paths followed by the majestic herd.

The Eastern elk is native to Michigan, and in pre-settlement times elk roamed the forests throughout the Lower Peninsula. But the intense logging of the 19th century quickly removed their habitat, and the herd began to dwindle. By 1877 the elk were gone for good, even from their stronghold in the Pigeon River Country. This area was heavily logged between 1860 and 1910, and all that remained when the lumbermen left were open fields of stumps and

slash. An era of uncontrolled forest fires followed. Some attempted to farm this rugged land, but when they were unsuccessful, ownership reverted to the state.

In 1919 Pigeon River Country State Forest was established. Reforestation began, and at the depth of the Great Depression the Civilian Conservation Corps constructed a huge log lodge 13 miles east of Vanderbilt as the forest headquarters. It became a monument to their tree-planting efforts. The forest came back, and so did the elk. Conservationists had made several attempts to reintroduce the species in the early 1900s, but failed until seven were transplanted from Yellowstone National Park to a spot near Wolverine in 1918. By 1927 the herd had multiplied to 500, and by 1960 there were more than 1,500.

During the following decade, Pigeon River Country became a raging battlefield. Oil and gas deposits were found under the south central portions of the forest, and early exploration and development had a devastating impact on wild-

life. So did poaching of elk, which was rampant at the time. In 1974 alone, 45 animals were illegally shot. The next year, the herd population was estimated at only 200.

The resulting public outcry pitted environmentalists and conservationists against developers and the oil industry over the future of the forest. After a lengthy string of court cases, legislative actions, and corporate compromises, a settlement was reached that satisfied few and allowed closely constrained removal of gas and oil. Meanwhile, new elk management techniques implemented in 1972 took hold, and the herd began a second comeback, growing to 700 animals in 1983 and breaking 1,000 two years later.

More problems besieged Pigeon River Country. Uncontrolled use of off-road vehicles was tearing up the landscape, and in 1985 the beloved log headquarters that overlooked the Pigeon River for half a century burnt to the ground. Both problems were resolved in 1990, when strict limits were placed on ORVs, and

LEFT: *A bull elk in the Pigeon River Country State Forest. The Michigan herd, re-introduced in 1918, now numbers over 1,000.*

RIGHT: *A male spring peeper singing from his perch on the edge of a pond.*

members of the Michigan Civilian Conservation Corps duplicated the effort of their forefathers with red pine cut from the surrounding forests.

Wild Michigan? Most assuredly.

Heavily forested once again and as rugged as ever, Pigeon River Country attracts outdoor enthusiasts from around the state for a variety of reasons. Within the area are seven campgrounds—small, rustic facilities tucked away on river bends and isolated lakes. Twenty-seven miles of horse trails and 60 miles of foot trails wind through a terrain of steep ridges and hills unmatched anywhere in the Lower Peninsula. One trail, the Shingle Mill Pathway, is an 11-mile loop along the Pigeon River that for many becomes a wilderness ski trip during the winter.

In 1985, Pigeon River Country was selected as the first site for reintroducing the pine marten in the Lower Peninsula. Other wildlife species that thrive here include black bear, bobcat, coyote, otter, grouse, woodcock, and the bald eagle.

But they all take a back seat to the elk.

Although a few live to 20 years of age, most elk have a lifespan of under 10 years. Grasses and plants are their main food source, but during deep snow cover they will browse on the twigs and stems of trees and shrubs. An adult can easily consume 25 pounds of grasses and plants during a day, an amount three times the consumption of an average adult deer. Elk are less susceptible to winter starvation than deer. Their huge build, generally four times the size of a trophy buck, makes them far less restricted by heavy snow.

Calves are born in late May and early June, and twins are rare. The newborn weighs 20 to 30 pounds at birth, and the mother will stay away from other elk until the calf is two to three weeks old. At that point cows, young bulls, and calves concentrate into large groups. Often, a few cows will baby-sit for as many as 20 calves while their mothers go off to graze.

Bulls grow their antlers every spring, drop them by the following March or April, and generally spend summer in small groups of five or six. By August they begin polishing their antlers for the fall rut, when they gather 15 to 20 cows—sometimes as many as 30—for the breeding season. Dominant bulls aggressively drive their weaker opponents away, using a low, whistling sound to issue challenges or mark territories.

Their mating call marks the season of bugling in northern Michigan, and it's the reason thousands of elk watchers arrive at Pigeon River Country every fall.

Although elk can be sighted all year, during summer they head for the thick underbrush of the forest to escape the heat, and in winter they gravitate to logging operations and clear-cut areas where they find an abundance of young, woody sprouts. The prime time for viewing elk,

Above: A winter sun emerges over Lake Huron near Rogers City. For those who are awake, the sunrises over the Great Lake are just as spectacular as the renowned Lake Michigan sunsets.

then, is from early September through mid-October, when the bulls bugle to form their harems.

There are fields and meadows scattered throughout the state forest, but three sites are posted as designated elk viewing areas:

—Eight miles east of Vanderbilt on Sturgeon Valley Road, right before you cross the Pigeon River.

—Along County Road 622, 18 miles east of Gaylord and a mile east of Meridian Line Road.

—Along Osmun Road, four miles north of the new state forest headquarters, reached by departing north from Sturgeon Valley Road onto Twin Lakes Road.

These grassy meadows are the focal points for elk during the rut, and the best times to sight them are dawn and dusk—especially in the final hour before dark. Elk watchers, like their counterparts in birding, equip themselves with binoculars to avoid disrupting the harems by trying to get a closer look.

For many elk watchers, the "wild" aspect of the encounter is diminished by crowds, so they make their trip in the middle of the week. They stop at state forest headquarters and inquire about more secluded viewing areas—meadows without signs. "Go to a viewing area on the weekend and you'll think everybody is out there with you," said one state biologist.

Even so, if you're quiet, still, and most of all, patient, you'll eventually experience what many believe is Michigan's most impressive encounter with wildlife. Susan did. On Saturday morning, her group returned to sight a herd of 15 elk, including two bulls with huge racks. As the elk drifted back into the woods, one bull started bugling. "It was a very high pitch. I would have never known it was an elk," she said.

Not living in New Hampshire, she wouldn't have.

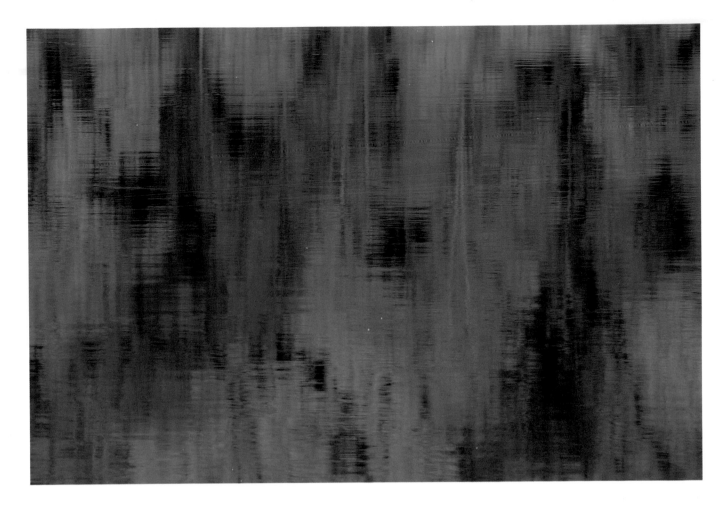

ABOVE: *Fall colors reflected in Pete's Lake in Alger County. Located south of Munising in the Hiawatha National Forest, the lake features a rustic campground maintained by the U.S. Forest Service.*

Gene,
Thanks for attending the
Denver seminar, Good-luck!
John Serlach
Nov 10, 1994

LEFT: *A red maple leaf is trapped in the icy grasp of a stand of spotted knapweed.*

Lake Huron State Parks

*M*ichael said he wanted to visit the old Indian chief. "Negwegon" doesn't quite roll off the tongue of most five-year-olds, but after our first trip there my son never forgot the wild ride we took to reach the area, the golden beaches we found there, or the fact that the park honors a famous Chippewa Chief.

So one day out of the blue he asked me, "When can we go back to that Indian chief place?"

We went back.

Perhaps the most unusual state park in the Lower Peninsula and without a doubt the most remote, Negwegon is a virtually undeveloped tract, visited for the most part by locals lucky enough to know about it and a few lost tourists who stumble into it. The 1,800-acre preserve on Lake Huron can only be reached by following a rough dirt road covered with mounds of drifting sand and sliced by the deep ruts of spinning tires.

On maps, it's labeled Sand Hill Road, and that should tell you something. It's the Baja 1000 with trees, only I wasn't driving a four-wheel-drive pickup with a roller bar.

Michael loved it. And when we reached the state park sign on the gravel entrance drive, I said a little prayer ("Oh Lord, please get me back") and Michael said, "We sure must be a long ways from anywhere."

Left: A sand wolf spider in Negwegon State Park. The remote park is located north of Harrisville along Lake Huron.

We sure were. Negwegon was established in 1962 as Alpena State Park, but two years later Hazlett Kramer, a resident on nearby Hubbard Lake, questioned its name. Such a remote, wild place deserved something better, so the 70-year-old conservationist began campaigning to rename the park.

For six years she made long trips to Lansing to address the Michigan Natural Resources Commission, attended meetings, and wrote dozens of letters—all in an effort to honor Native Americans by naming the park after a Chippewa chief who remained loyal to the U.S. during the War of 1812. Her persistence paid off. In 1970, Alpena State Park became Negwegon State Park.

Most of the park is a mix of upland hardwoods, marshes, and other low-lying areas that could be any forest in northern Michigan. But not the shoreline. Many believe the most beautiful and isolated beaches on Lake Huron lie within this park. Words like "paradise" have been used to describe Negwegon's 6.5-mile shoreline, which includes stretches of wide, sugary beaches in remote bays, lined by towering pines and closed in by rocky points and spits.

The first time we arrived, we didn't make it beyond the beaches. From the parking area, we walked 20 yards past a yellow gate and a water spigot, then broke out of the trees onto a crescent-moon beach. It was a half-mile long, and its golden sand gently sloped into the turquoise waters of Lake Huron. We were the only ones there.

ABOVE: Round-lobed hepatica in full bloom in
Negwegon. Along with its pristine beaches,
the park offers extensive hardwood forests.

RIGHT: Paper birch trees frame a spring
sky. The white-bark trees are found
throughout Negwegon State Park.

Paradise.

The fact that there are such places along
Lake Huron surprises many people. Every summer thousands flock to Lake Michigan, the Gold
Coast of our state, to enjoy the widest beaches,
the tallest dunes, and the most spectacular sunsets in the Midwest. But the sunrise side of
Michigan also has beaches, though not as many;
dunes, though not as impressive; and state parks,
never as crowded.

There's Port Crescent. To historians, Port
Crescent was a thriving lumber town in the mid-
1800s, known for its salt wells and good docks.
To families on the east side of the state, Port
Crescent is a 565-acre state park that includes
three miles of almost-pure white beach along
Saginaw Bay. But to hikers, this preserve is a

tract of wind-blown dunes and wooded hills high
enough to provide sweeping panoramas of the
bay, of the shoreline, of the marshy valley carved
by the Pinnebog River. In the flatland of the
Thumb, most people are stunned to discover
such overlooks.

There's Tawas Point. Occasionally referred
to as the "Cape Cod of the Midwest," Tawas
Point State Park is 185 acres at the end of a long,
sandy spit. There's more than two miles of white,
sandy beach that borders the blue waters of Lake
Huron on one side and forms the north end of
Tawas Bay on the other. The spit is crowned by a
lighthouse. The Cape Cod comparison may be
debatable, but its reputation as a haven for
birders is not. During the annual migration, the
spit becomes a natural landfall for birds crossing

Saginaw Bay, and a check list published by the park indicates that 205 species have been spotted. On the beaches, you can see Caspian terns and Bonaparte's gulls, along with shorebirds such as red knots, whimbrels, and even the rare piping plover. Inland ponds attract loons, flocks of mergansers, and other waterfowl, while warblers, flycatchers, and hummingbirds feed among the willow thickets and sand cherry shrubs at the end of the spit.

There's Thompson's Harbor. Established in 1988, the 5,247-acre state park is 20 miles north of Alpena, and is still an undeveloped tract. The scenic appeal of Thompson's Harbor lies in its limestone points and in beaches that fashion a series of harbors, shallow beach pools, and more than seven miles of cobble beach, all unique for the western side of Lake Huron. Low-lying dunes border the shoreline, most of them stabilized by grasses, bearberry, and low junipers; others feature blowouts of bare sand that have been carved by steady winds off the lake. Wild-

flowers are abundant in Thompson's Harbor, ranging from the large, bright-orange wood lilies to the world's largest population of dwarf lake iris, federally designated as a threatened plant.

There's P.H. Hoeft and Harrisville. Located near Rogers City and Harrisville, these state parks are noted for their forested campgrounds, lakefront sites, and beautiful, wide beaches, where campers set up lawn chairs and spend an August afternoon watching the lake freighters sail past on the horizon.

And then there's Negwegon. Find it if you can.

The second time we did, I resisted the temptation to kick off my boots and lie on the beach. This time, my son and I were determined to reach South Point, so we departed the north end of the parking lot along an overgrown two-track road into a forest of beech, maple, and paper birch. In the beginning, Lake Huron was out of sight as we tiptoed around a few wet areas.

But in the next two miles, we caught a

glimpse of the lake, passed through an enchanting stand of paper birch whose white trunks were framed by a deep blue sky, and came to a junction with another old two-track. This one veered to the east through a grassy clearing, and we followed it, hoping to reach the lake. We quickly returned to the woods, but it was evident we were on South Point. We could see water between the trees on both sides of us. The point marks the southern end of Thunder Bay and, based on digs here, archaeologists say it was probably a traditional resting place for Indians paddling the Great Lake.

Just as we emerged from the trees, a bald eagle took off and soared high over Lake Huron. Only when it was out of sight did we take our eyes off the sky and look at the view. It was unbelievable—a magnificent, 360-degree panorama of Lake Huron. The view to the north revealed miles of shoreline all the way back to the water towers of Alpena, along with two islands—Bird Island and, farther out, Scarecrow Island, which is preserved as a national refuge.

To the south was the jagged shoreline of this incredible state park. We stood on the tip and could see all the way back to that crescent moon bay whose golden sand had hypnotized us on our first trip out, preventing this hike to the Point.

Perhaps the best reason for hiking to South Point is not to see the beautiful beaches, but to understand the true value of this park. In recent years, more attention has been focused on Negwegon, as a controversy has raged over its future development. Some area businesses, eyeing the summer crush of humanity experienced along Lake Michigan, want Sand Hill Road paved and a modern campground built in the park, to draw more tourists and their dollars.

Others believe what Kramer, with her incredible insight, knew three decades earlier—that Negwegon is too priceless to be developed; that it's a rare piece of real estate worth keeping natural and pristine.

Hopefully, those who cast the final votes on Negwegon's future will not push for such conveniences as electrical hook-ups for trailers, bathhouses, or refreshment stands that draw flocks of tourists and drive away the eagles. Crowded beaches are everywhere in Michigan. Negwegon's greatest asset is not its beaches, as beautiful as they are, but the remoteness you feel while viewing Lake Huron from South Point.

Isle Royale National Park

A twig broke.

The noise pierced the air, and I instinctively froze. I could hear something out there, but I couldn't see because my head was buried inside a kayak I was portaging from Lake Richie on Isle Royale National Park. So I stopped, lifted the boat partially off my sore shoulders, and peeked from under the gunwales of the cockpit.

Sheesh. A moose in the middle of the trail. Not just any moose, but a bull with a rack so large that every ranger in the park could have hung a hat on it, and there'd be room left over for a few coats.

He was tall and he was wide—so wide that trees on both sides of the path were touching him. And he was looking at me—no question about that. We stood on the trail with only 20 yards separating us. We probably would have stood there for a while, but the weight of the kayak began to make my shoulders throb. So I finally broke the silence and said the only thing I ever heard anybody say to a moose.

"Hey, Bullwinkle, move it."

The bull swung his head slowly. What was above my head was considerably larger than what was above his. But his rack seemed like a much more permanent fixture, so it was I who began to retreat.

If just portaging a 16-foot boat down a narrow, wooded trail is hard, walking backward with

the boat is impossible. I banged into three trees and wandered into the brush, thoroughly tangling the rudder and its cables in some pencil-thin saplings. The bull finally moved. He headed into the woods and skirted around the path. He had no time, apparently, for a guy who couldn't handle his own rack.

· · · · · · · ·

Man meets moose. On this island in the stormy northwest corner of Lake Superior, such encounters are a daily occurrence from May, when visitors begin arriving, until November, when the 210-square-mile preserve closes for winter—the only national park in the U.S. that does so.

Between spring and fall, some 15,000 people venture to the park, and the vast majority of them—park officials estimate almost 12,000—are backcountry users. Day hikers, backpackers, canoeists, kayakers and others come looking for wilderness. The island is their sought-after haven from the daily routines and urban sprawl back at home, if only for a week or two.

Although small by national park standards, Isle Royale offers a greater variety of wilderness adventure than many parks twice its size. It's 45 miles long from end to end and 8.5 miles wide at its broadest point. Its backbone, the Greenstone Ridge, climbs three times to more than 1,300 feet. Mount Desor is the highest point on the island at 1,394 feet.

There are no roads on Isle Royale, thus no cars, no traffic lights, no rush hours, no sets of golden arches. Instead, the island is laced with 165 miles of trails—forested avenues ranging from a well-defined and level path to the Minong Ridge Trail, which is notorious for being little more than an up-and-down struggle over a bare rock ridge. You can day hike from the park hotel at Rock Harbor and be back in time for a lake trout dinner at the hotel's restaurant. Or you can undertake a two-week trek that circles the island and never backtrack a single step.

You can also paddle, working a canoe through a series of portages that connect nine lakes with coves, harbors, and narrow, fiord-like bays in an area at the park's east end known as the Five Fingers. Or you can take a sea kayak to the rugged outside coast of the island and marvel at the power of a four-foot swell or the endless blue horizon that is Lake Superior.

The symbol of Isle Royale wilderness and the subject of books, magazine articles, and theses is the wolf, but that's a bit ironic for those returning home on the ferry every summer. You read about the wolves and their struggle to survive on the island, but when visiting the park it's the moose you see and remember long after the trip is over. An encounter with a seven-foot, 1,000-pound animal is not forgotten any time soon. "If you want to see a moose," said a park biologist, "this is the place to be."

That's because there are so many. The 1990 aerial census put the population at just above 1,200 animals, giving Isle Royale a moose density of three to five times higher than any other mainland area in North America. By comparison, the rest of Michigan's moose population, living mostly in the central part of the Upper Peninsula, totals between 250 and 300. Throughout much of the island there are perhaps 1.2 moose per square mile, but in areas like Feldtmann Lake at the west end, biologists have recorded densities as high as 4.2.

Unlike the U.P. herd, which arrived by truck

in 1985 from Ontario, Isle Royale moose reached the island by swimming the 15 miles from Canada. The emigration occurred at a time when moose on the mainland were faced with growing competition for food. Isle Royale's first moose arrived around 1900, finding an abundance of shrubs to feed on and no natural predators. Others migrated here, and the new herd exploded in numbers. Some estimate that as many as 3,000 moose inhabited the island by 1930, when the population began to fluctuate wildly.

A large number starved to death in the winter of 1933, but the fire of 1936 burned 20 percent of the island, creating vast open areas for small trees and shrubs to take root. This new source of "moose salad," as biologists call it, caused another dramatic upswing in the population.

Nature's answer to the problem was the wolf, and a handful of the predators crossed frozen Lake Superior in 1949, finding a ready food supply on the island. The two species kept each other in check, in a classic example of the ancient predator-prey relationship. But in 1980, the cycle fell out of sync.

That year, biologists were stunned when they recorded an all-time high of 50 wolves in five territorial packs on Isle Royale. Just two years later the number crashed to a low of 12, and in 1990 there were still only 12 to 15 animals. Many feared that the days of the eastern timber wolf on Isle Royale were numbered, and a lack of genetic variability was blamed. There were so few wolves that in-breeding had resulted, and the packs' reproductive rate had dropped. "They're not so much dying," one biologist said. "They're just not reproducing."

The number of moose has also declined, after peaking at more than 1,600 in 1988. Biologists believe that the 25 percent drop in the population was caused more by winter ticks and sparse winter forage than by wolves.

Still, the abundance of moose on the island is astounding. Backcountry visitors who take to the trails and water routes of the park will see signs of moose everywhere. Trails are littered with nuggets and other moose scat. The large, pear-shaped prints crowd the edge of every stream and swamp. In clearings, every small fir or aspen has been nibbled clean by hungry moose, leaving little more than a forest of sticks.

During the rutting season from mid-September to late October, you can hear the moose. Visitors have been known to spend half the night awake in their tents, listening to moose trotting after each other through deserted campgrounds

Above: Sunrise over Rock Harbor on Isle Royale. The national park in the northwest corner of Lake Superior is the only one in the country that closes down entirely for the winter. The visitor's season extends from April through October.

or bulls bellowing their mating call (more of a snort, really) into the early hours of the morning.

Eventually, if you spend enough time hiking the island's trails or paddling its waters, you'll meet a moose face to face, so to speak, in what many say is the best wildlife encounter that Michigan has to offer. Spotting the ungainly animal in the backcountry is easy. Moose are not skittish, and they tolerate people quite well.

In the summer, moose often feed on aquatic plants in streams, lakes, and protected coves. The best way to encounter one, a situation that allows both parties to feel safe, is from a canoe or kayak. You'll spot the moose from a distance, take a couple of good strokes, and quietly put down the paddles to pick up your camera. You can get within 20 or 30 yards before a feeding cow will know you're there. Even then, she'll finish off what she was eating and nonchalantly climb up the shore, pausing to turn around and study you as intently as you're studying her. You'll be only 10 or 15 yards away when she finally disappears for good into the woods.

In the fall, park rangers say moose should be treated with extra caution—especially the bulls, which can be extremely temperamental during the rut. Many backpackers rate this 1,000-pound animal the most dangerous in North America, and consider it the source of a greater number of unpleasant confrontations than the bear.

Most visitors arrive at the park nervous about encountering a moose, but without fail they're disappointed if they don't. The proof is audible on the long ferry ride back to the mainland, as departing backpackers swap tales and adventures. It's never the long climb to Mount Siskiwit, the two-mile portage to Lake Richie, or the blisters earned on the crest of the Minong Ridge that made the island seem so desolate and wild and memorable to these visitors.

It was their five-minute encounter with a moose.

OVERLEAF: The frozen Lake Superior shoreline within Pictured Rocks National Lakeshore. In winter the park becomes a paradise for Nordic skiers, snowshoers, and ice climbers who like to scale frozen waterfalls.

Porcupine Mountains Wilderness

There was a snafu with the cabin keys.

Somebody forgot to pick up the set for the eight-bunk cabin on Mirror Lake before we left on our backpacking trip into the Porcupine Mountains. Only we didn't discover it until we'd reached the six-bunk cabin at the mouth of the Big Carp River . . . seven miles from where we hiked in, ten miles from where we left the other vehicle, and a four-mile walk just to reach the nearest road.

That startling discovery gave us the same sinking feeling a skier has after twisting an ankle miles from the trailhead. In the middle of Michigan's most rugged corner, we were without tents, sleeping pads, or the key to the next cabin.

Time to make do. A couple from Chicago was gracious enough to let us spend an extra night in the cabin on the Big Carp River, and the next day we did a ten-mile trek through the heart of this 61,000-acre state park, carrying full packs in a driving rain.

From the shores of Lake Superior at 611 feet, we marched across the Porkies, at one point reaching 1,620 feet only to descend again several hundred feet to Mirror Lake. We ended the day by climbing to a parking lot near Summit Peak, the highest point in the park at 1,958 feet. Between the long climbs and knee-bending

descents, we crossed streams without bridges, slogged through stretches of mud that swallowed our boots, and paused to catch our breath beneath the towering trunks of maples and hemlocks 300 years old.

"It's either mountains or mudholes out here," said one member of our party, and as the cold rain dripped down our face and our shoulders throbbed from the weight of 30- or 40-pound packs, we all agreed. This place was rugged enough to be called mountains, remote enough to stay wild, unforgiving to those who come unprepared, and very much worthy of its middle name. Porcupine Mountains Wilderness State Park is indeed a wilderness.

"There are certainly more remote places than this," said Ron Welton, the park's longtime manager. "In relation to northern Canada or Alaska, maybe we don't qualify as wilderness. But in terms of the Midwest, we certainly do. It's pretty rugged country. If you're not going uphill, you're going downhill, and if you're not going downhill, you're going through mud."

It has always been that way for those who have endured the steep climbs. As early as 1750 B.C., Indians were wandering into the Porcupine Mountains during the summer to mine copper. Using fire and water to rapidly heat, cool, and then fracture boulders, they pounded out the metal and shaped it into tools, ornaments, and projectile points. According to estimates, ancient miners extracted between 500

Left: A rocky stretch of Lake Superior shore found within the Porcupine Mountains Wilderness State Park. The park contains 25 miles of Great Lake shoreline.

LEFT: *An evening primrose in brilliant bloom. Cultivated primroses are often used as ornamental garden flowers.*

ABOVE: *Downstream from Manabezho Falls in the Presque Isle River. The river flows over several spectacular waterfalls within Porcupine Mountains State Park.*

million and a billion pounds of copper from an area that included the Porkies, Isle Royale, and the Keweenaw Peninsula. They then traded it throughout North America.

The first white settlements consisted of only a few isolated fur trading posts until 1840. That's when Douglass Houghton published his geological survey of the western Upper Peninsula, triggering a copper stampede to both the Porcupine Mountains and the Keweenaw area.

Despite uncovering the Ontonagon Boulder, a 3,708-pound nugget of copper that today rests in the Smithsonian Institution, miners quickly exhausted the copper veins in the Porkies. The silver mines that followed never paid out, and after loggers cut the trees along the Lake Superior shoreline, they passed up the rugged interior of

the Porkies for more accessible tracts elsewhere.

Thus the interior remained unmolested by miners, loggers, and other entrepreneurs, and was so pristine that in the late 1930s the federal government designated the Porkies a potential site for the next national park. The plans were abandoned by the financially strapped Congress at the start of World War II, but when the wartime demand for lumber renewed the loggers' interest in the interior timber, concerned citizens and the state stepped in.

Global conflict notwithstanding, this distant corner of Michigan, harboring the largest stand of virgin maple and hemlock between the Rockies and the Adirondacks, was too precious to be stripped. A push for preservation of the Porkies resulted in state park status in 1945.

"It was almost a national park, and it really is a national park-quality resource," said Welton. "Few state parks have the resource base that the Porkies have."

Or the dimensions. Although the majority of the 500,000 annual visitors never venture beyond the Lake of the Clouds overlook, a spectacular vista of a lake surrounded by ridges and escarpments, this park is much more than one frequently photographed viewing point.

Michigan's largest state park is 26 miles long, and 10 miles across at its widest point. Along with peaks that top 1,900 feet, the Porkies contain 25 miles of Lake Superior shoreline, four lakes, entire rivers, trout streams choked with spawning salmon in the fall, nine waterfalls that are named, and dozens of falls that are not.

More than 90 miles of footpaths wind through the heart of this wilderness. The longest is the Lake Superior Trail, stretching for 16 miles along the lakeshore. Many say the most scenic trek in the Upper Peninsula is the hike along the four-mile Escarpment Trail, which gives way to vistas of sheer cliffs and panoramas of Lake of the Clouds from Cuyahoga and Cloud peaks.

But of all the trails in the park, the path down the Big Carp River best mirrors the diversity of the Porkies. It begins near the Lake of the Clouds overlook and parallels for two miles the western half of the escarpment, offering outstanding views of Big Carp River Valley and the rugged interior of the park.

The trail then descends into the valley, passes old Lafayette Mine, and finally crosses the Big Carp River at the site of one of three Adirondack shelters where backpackers can find a roof, bunks, and a table for the night. From this point on, the nine-mile trail swings to the north and follows the river on its course to Lake Superior. Along the way, you can pause on the edge of the gorge to take in the wonder of Shining Cloud Falls, which thunders downward between sheer walls of rock. You end the trip on the shores of the largest Great Lake, whose surf in November can be as impressive as the mist off Shining Cloud.

With mountain views, stone canyons, thundering waterfalls, and a Great Lake, it's a bit ironic that the feature most valued by many park visitors is man-made—a group of more than a dozen rustic cabins scattered throughout the backcountry.

The cabins range in size from two to eight bunks. They contain woodburning stoves,

tables, benches, and a log book in which to jot down tales and tips for the next group of overnighters. Cooking and eating utensils, an ax and saws, and some of the hardest mattresses you'll ever sleep on are also provided.

But in the middle of wilderness, when it's snowing in September or raining in April, there's nothing prettier—not even the escarpment view of Lake of the Clouds—than the warm glow in your cabin's windows, or the spiral of smoke drifting out of its chimney.

And in the end, these homes away from home truly make the Porkies unique. You can find black bears roaming the night, eagles soaring overhead, and trophy steelhead trout elsewhere. But this state park, claims its staff, is the only one in the Midwest with a network of cabins along its trails—rustic log structures accessible only on foot.

Some, like the new Gitche Gumme Cabin, require a mere five-minute stroll down a level trail. Others, like the three units at Big Carp River, are reached after a nine-, seven-, or four-mile trek, depending on where you begin. There are also cabins overlooking Lake Superior, cabins on Lake of the Clouds, cabins near waterfalls, and a cabin on serene Lily Pond, all for the price of a little boot leather (and $25 a night).

The majority of visitors use the cabins as a means of exploring the park, staying at a different one each night. Others book them as a base camp for deer season, and some families believe renting a rustic cabin is the only way to celebrate Thanksgiving.

"They hike the turkey in and everything," said Welton.

But the popularity of the cabins is almost as legendary as the mudholes along Correction

Line Trail or the climb to Government Peak. Many are reserved a year and a half in advance. Lotteries are held for certain cabins during hunting season, and an empty cabin anywhere in the park on any night between April and December is unheard of.

The demand is easy to understand. You may have to walk in, but you don't have sleep on the ground, and that small concession is enough to open up the wilderness—even a wilderness as rugged as the Porkies—to some of the most unlikely people.

The log books are filled with the testimonies of self-surprised individuals.

"I'm not a woodsmen, nor a person who really gets close to nature," wrote one Wisconsin visitor to the Big Carp River Cabin. "Roughing it, to me, is staying at the Holiday Inn when I had reservations at the Hilton."

And yet he was out there.

LEFT: *The bridge crossing the Presque Isle River at the western edge of the Porcupine Mountains Wilderness State Park.*

OVERLEAF: *Autumn colors at Thornton Lake in the Upper Peninsula's Alger County.*

McCormick Wilderness

$\mathcal{F}$red Rydholm was our *negaunee*. At the side of County Road 607, he strapped on his snowshoes and entered the deep snow of the McCormick Wilderness, and we quickly did the same.

"To the Indians, *negaunee* meant 'one who leads,'" said the 67-year-old, retired science teacher and former mayor of Marquette.

So Rydholm took off into the pines and hardwoods, sliding his bear paw snowshoes one over the other through snow that was two feet deep here, four over there. The rest of us followed him, keeping one eye on the Big Foot-like tracks he was leaving and the other on the incredible scenery that surrounded us here in this 16,850-acre, federally declared wilderness.

We couldn't have found a better *negaunee*. Rydholm, who wandered the tract as a youth and still maintains a cabin nearby, was part guide, part historian, and part naturalist, but most of all he was the colorful character you'd expect a backwoodsman and fourth-generation Yooper to be.

"The bugs aren't too bad here during the summer," said Rydholm. "Now, in 1942, they were bad. The gnats were so bad that year they blackened the sun."

"It's getting deep here, Fred," someone said. "And I'm not talking about the snow." Rydholm laughed at the *cheechakoes* behind him.

LEFT: *Fall in the Ottawa National Forest, located in the western half of Michigan's Upper Peninsula.*

Such is the man who weaves a trail through the history of this wilderness.

After loggers cleared most of the tract's white pine in the early 1900s, Cyrus McCormick, who invented the reaping machine and made his fortune with International Harvester, and Cyrus Bentley, the chief attorney for the company, purchased the area. But they made the buy only after McCormick consulted a professor at Harvard University. "They picked this place out because it's one of the greatest watersheds in the country," said Rydholm. "Look at a map and pick out all the lakes, rivers, and ponds. You won't find another place like it."

The wilderness was a family retreat for the next three generations of McCormicks. They maintained five camps here, but the most impressive lodge was at White Deer Lake, built on a small island a hundred yards offshore.

"To get from the shore to the island, they had a raft with an Armstrong motor," said Rydholm, who then paused with a big Yooper grin.

"An Armstrong motor, Fred?"

"Sure was. You had to pull yourself out and pull yourself back in."

Rydholm laughed, and with every step into the wilderness more McCormick lore spilled out of our *negaunee*.

There was a time, it seems, when McCormick was so worried about lightning striking the beloved pines surrounding his island lodge

that, in 1918, when copper was already heavily rationed due to the war, he had every tree equipped with a copper lightning rod.

There were McCormick's amenities, such as an $80,000 woodshed and a floating tennis court. "The floating golf ball was invented for this place," said Rydholm. "They would tee off into the lake, then send out a kid in a boat to pick the balls up."

Then there was the Bentley Trail. No tall tale here or Yooper exaggeration. The pathway was completed in 1905, and stretched from White Deer Lake to the Huron Mountain Club, an equally exclusive wilderness retreat organized in 1899 along Lake Superior to the north.

In 1942 Rydholm was an 18-year-old working the summer at the Club. An old guide named Indian Jim Dakota told him about the trail, which was hidden by that time beneath a growth of saplings and brush from lack of use.

Three years later Rydholm entered the McCormick Tract for the first time, and eventually he began guiding fishermen and hikers into

the rugged corner of the Upper Peninsula. In 1949 he bought what was known as the Halfway Cabin. The rustic cabin was located where the Bentley Trail winds through Yellow Dog Plains, halfway between the tract and the club. Rydholm retraced the lost trail, cleared out the brush, marked it, and has since made the trip on foot from one wilderness to the other more than 200 times.

Today the Huron Mountain Club is as exclusive as ever, but the McCormick Tract is no longer a family hideaway. Cyrus' retreat, including his island pines, became part of the Ottawa National Forest when his grandson, Gordon McCormick, donated the estate to the U.S. Forest Service upon his death in 1967.

Twenty years later it was designated as wilderness when Congress passed the Michigan Wilderness Act. The act itself provoked a heated debate throughout the state. Many questioned whether areas such as the Nordhouse Dunes in the Lower Peninsula were true wilderness. No one, however, questioned the McCormick Tract.

The preserve covers 27 square miles of forested land straddling the divide between the Lake Superior and Lake Michigan watersheds. There are 18 lakes in the tract, as well as the headwaters of four rivers. The Huron, Yellow Dog, and Dead rivers flow north into Lake Superior, and the Peshekee heads to the south.

The tract is rugged, with a terrain ranging from rocky cliffs and outcrops to glacier-scoured hills, including one that tops off at 1,890 feet. Some of the most impressive, hardest-to-reach waterfalls in the state are on the Yellow Dog, and are rarely seen. McCormick is bordered to the northeast by the Huron Mountains, while less than ten miles to the west are Michigan's highest peaks—Mt. Curwood at 1,978 feet, and Mt. Avon at 1,979.

Between the hills and bluffs are swamps, bogs, and muskegs that rim the lakes and streams. These lakes are more like those found farther north on the Canadian Shield than those in the Upper Peninsula, due to low fish populations. But other wildlife thrives in this wilderness isolated from the masses. Moving through the mixed northern hardwoods and lowland conifer forests are whitetail deer, foxes, otters, mink, snowshoe hares, and the endangered loon. Beavers abound, as is evident from the active and abandoned beaver dams on most streams and rivers. McCormick also harbors bald eagles, the bulk of Michigan's recently transplanted moose herd, black bears, and possibly wolves which, many believe, are slowly migrating into the Upper Peninsula from northern Minnesota and across Wisconsin.

But perhaps the most stunning encounter you'll experience within the tract is not sighting a bear or even a moose. Rather, it's the experience of stumbling across one of the small pockets of virgin white pine. The 300-year-old trees are located among rugged rock outcrops, and were too much trouble for loggers to harvest.

"The logger cut most of the pine, but not all of it," said Rydholm. "Some of the biggest pines in the world can be found here."

A trickle of people find their way into the heart of the tract, searching for its most priceless quality—the feeling of solitude in a seemingly unspoiled world. At one time more than 100 miles of trails criss-crossed the area, but they have long since fallen into disuse. Today it takes an old-timer like Rydholm to locate even a portion of them.

Canoeing opportunities are almost non-existent, due to the lengthy portages between lakes, and cross-country skiing is limited by the snow depths. Most anglers bypass the area, and only a limited number of backpackers, smothering themselves in bug juice, take to the trail in June and July. Many—Rydholm included—feel that the best mode of travel is by snowshoes and the best time to trek the McCormick is in winter, when there are no gnats blackening the sky.

"You've just done something that 99 percent of the people in Michigan have never done," said Rydholm. "You've snowshoed into the McCormick Wilderness."

That solitude was upon us from the minute we crossed a bridge over the Peshekee River near C.R. 607 and began following an old road to White Deer Lake. The three-mile road, now the only posted trail in the wilderness, passes Baraga Stream and then skirts a series of rocky bluffs that tower 50 or 60 feet above. It swings past Camp Lake, eventually reaching White Deer Lake and all that remains of the McCormick Lodge—a few stone foundations.

Following the trail is easy, even in winter, as it's an unmistakable avenue through the trees. If you wander off, though, you'd better have a compass and topographical map. Even Rydholm will attest to that. There are so few winter travelers in the tract that Rydholm was shocked once to come across another set of snowshoe tracks. He began to follow them.

"After 20 minutes, two sets of tracks appeared," said Rydholm with a grin. "And I thought, 'Oh-oh.' "

Even a *negaunee* like Rydholm can get turned around in the McCormick Wilderness.

Pictured Rocks National Lakeshore

When we arrived at Munising Falls, the first stop on any visit to the Pictured Rocks National Lakeshore, we were behind a tour group. Two loaded buses pulled into the parking area and threw open their doors. What followed was nothing short of a stampede. More than 100 tourists rushed down the short path toward the falls.

All these people and all this commotion gave me that same panic-stricken feeling I had while visiting Disney World. So when we continued to Miner's Castle, the most famous rock formation in the park, and saw those same tour buses in front of us, I stepped on the brakes.

I'd had enough group participation for the day. Instead, we parked at the trailhead for Miners Falls, situated just ahead of the famed nine-story monolith, and quickly entered the woods. Miners Falls Trail is a descent to an observation deck overlooking the cascade—a round-trip of only 1.2 miles with a staircase that's 77 steps down and 77 steps back up. But it's just demanding enough to keep tour groups at bay and provide you with a bit of natural beauty in a quiet setting, even during the busiest day in the park.

The secret to experiencing the wildness of Pictured Rocks lies in finding its uncrowded spots.

The National Lakeshore stretches for 42 miles along the south shore of Lake Superior,

Left: Munising Falls in the Pictured Rocks National Lakeshore is one of the most popular attractions in the state, partly because visitors can stroll behind the tumbling cascade.

between Munising and Grand Marais. Its widest point is three miles, and almost half of its inland boundary is a half-mile or less from the Great Lake. The park itself contains 33,500 acres, but a buffer zone of 37,850 acres has been set up to protect the famous shoreline and the area's watersheds.

Most of the land is covered with a mixture of northern hardwoods, pine, spruce, and fir. Tracts of sand dunes, wetlands, lakes, small ponds, many streams, and some of the most spectacular waterfalls in the state break up the green monotony of the forest. It's an incredibly diverse land blessed with stunning natural formations. Yet for the vast majority of visitors, Pictured Rocks is a three-hour boat ride out to Munising. They never actually set foot inside the park.

Michigan's most famous tour is a cruise along the Pictured Rocks, after which the park is named. Ten thousand years ago, melting glaciers left behind an exposed lakefront escarpment that stretches for 15 miles just northeast of Munising. Lake Superior's wicked nature has long since carved the Cambrian sandstone into stacks, arches, caves and promontories. The most famous is Miners Castle, the only one that can be viewed from land. But others, including Battleship Row, Grand Portal, and Colored Caves, are equally impressive from the surface of the lake.

The boat tour also allows you to study the *colors* of the cliffs, which are almost as impressive as the formations themselves. The Pictured

Lake Superior, the Lakeshore Trail is a three- to four-day trek along the edge of the Pictured Rocks, over the sands of Twelvemile Beach, and through the heart of the Grand Sable Dunes.

Other quiet spots are less ambitious but just as intriguing. One involves a hike along an over-grown access road from Hurricane Campground to Au Sable Point Light Station, an easy walk of only 1.5 miles. But on the way you can explore the remains of shipwrecks along the beach. If you're walking in November, when the skies are gray, the lake's powerful surf is crashing along the rocky shore, and there's a hint of snow in the air, you can feel the fear that must have seeped into the mind of every sailor who rounded this point at the turn of the century.

The stretch of Lake Superior from Munising to Whitefish Point, some 80 miles to the east, was known to sailors in the early 1900s as "the graveyard of the Great Lakes." The area was feared not only for its offshore reefs, but because a strong northwest wind could blow unob-structed across almost 200 miles of lake. The late-season gales and Lake Superior's extremely deep water often combined to create waves 20 to 30 feet high. More than 200 ships perished in this graveyard, including the *Edmund Fitzgerald*, which took its captain and crew of 28 to the bot-tom of the lake in 1975. Sailors who survived the wrecks often froze to death before rescuers could reach the desolate stretch of shore.

Even after the Au Sable Light Station was built in 1874, ships continued to run aground on the Au Sable Reef, including three whose re-mains are half-buried in the sandy beach. The first piece of wreckage is near the campground,

Rocks at times reach heights of 200 feet above the water, gradually intensifying in color due to the seepage of underlying minerals. Bands of brown, gold, and red change each hour with the setting sun. The Colored Caves formation is so red in late afternoon that Ojibwa Indians were sure their enemies had left war prisoners inside to be dashed to pieces.

Those who do venture into the park usually spend a few hours at Munising Falls and Miners Castle, perched on an overlook, then call it a day. What's left are the park's quiet spots. And there are many.

Ambitious visitors explore the backcountry by way of the park's Lakeshore Trail. The 42.8-mile footpath is part of the North Country Trail, which will someday stretch from North Dakota to New York. Many argue that this is the most scenic stretch of the 3,200-mile trail. Skirting

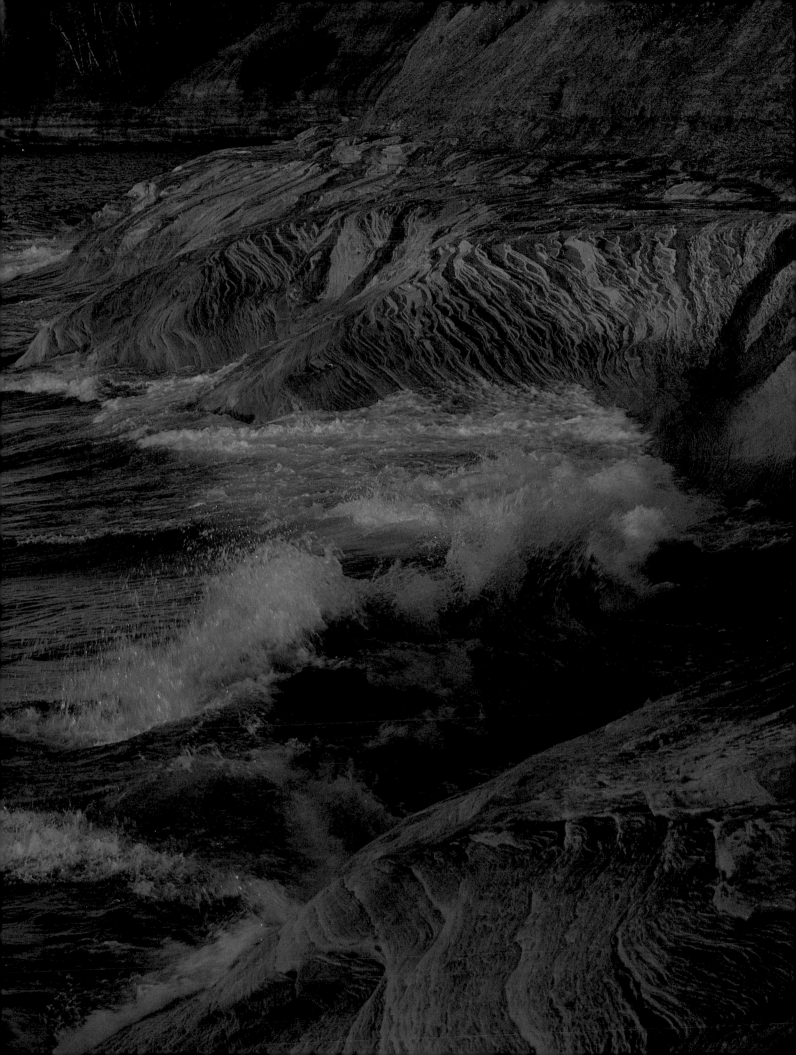

Above: An American goldfinch, a species that is frequently spotted in the Pictured Rocks National Lakeshore. The goldfinch is also known as the "wild canary" because of its color and melodic song.

Right: Miner's Castle in winter. The nine-story monolith is the most famous formation within the Pictured Rocks National Lakeshore.

20 yards offshore, but it's difficult to spot if there's any chop on the lake. Park staff members believe these timbers belong to the *Mary Jarecki*, a wooden-hulk freighter that ran aground in 1883, when the crew became disoriented in a thick fog and the ship hit the reef at full steam.

A mile up the trail, you arrive at a second "Shipwreck" sign that leads you back down to the beach to examine two more wrecks. Lying on the shore, half-buried in sand, are huge pieces of timber with the ironwork still protruding from them. The first ship is thought to be the remains of the *Gale Staples*, a Canadian wooden steamer that was built in 1881 and ran aground in 1918 with a full load of coal. Its crew spent a harrowing night aboard the battered ship before a Coast Guard surf boat from Grand Marais pulled them off. The second vessel was

the *Sitka*, a wooden steamer bound for Toledo with a load of ore when she was stranded on the reef in 1904. The howling gale broke her in half before the vessel could be pulled off.

Standing here in November, when there's not a soul around and the wind is whipping the trees on the bluff above and the waves are crashing among the ancient ribs of a keel, a shipwreck is not hard to imagine. Not hard at all.

Other escapes within the park include the trek out to Chapel Falls, which cascades 90 feet down a sandstone cliff into the narrow gorge that is Chapel Lake.

Or you can undertake a knee-bending climb across the Grand Sable Dunes to stand on the edge of a perched dune, 300 feet above Lake Superior, while viewing the Au Sable Light Station silhouetted against the water to the west.

ABOVE: Chapel Falls, surrounded by autumn colors. The cascade tumbles 90 feet down a sandstone cliff into Chapel Lake.

Then there's Miners Falls Trail. It's a trip to Miners River, a waterway that begins to the south near the town of Shingleton, and on its way to emptying into Lake Superior, passes over its namesake falls and through Miners Lake.

The area was first visited in 1771-72 by Englishman Alexander Henry, who arrived looking for "leaders"—indicators of mineral deposits. His party of geologists found one in the discolored water oozing from nearby bedrock, and named the waterway Miners River. It's one of those funny twists of history, because the area never did yield any valuable minerals. But today the trail to the falls is a priceless escape from crowds.

You begin in a northern mixed hardwood forest dominated by American beech whose gray bark in the fall, according to the interpretive brochure, resembles elephant legs. At one point you skirt the edge of a ridge, and in late fall when enough leaves have fallen, you can gaze down into a large basin, the setting for marshy Miners Lake, while on the horizon you see Lake Superior.

Eventually the path turns into a steep set of steps, often wet and a little slippery from the clouds of mist created by Miners Falls. But the descent is worth it. You end up at a small platform complete with benches, overlooking the thundering volume of water that comes roaring over an inland section of the Pictured Rocks escarpment.

The setting is a rocky gorge, with the tea-colored river outlined by the lush green of spruce, fir, cedar, and other conifers that thrive around the cascade. Far from the crowds above, we sat down on our private observation deck, enjoying a rainbow of hues reflected in the rising mist. We didn't get up to leave until a young family came struggling down the steps.

"It's all yours," I said, and began the trek back to our car.

OVERLEAF: The Pictured Rocks shoreline is part of an 80-mile stretch of Lake Superior known to sailors as "the Graveyard of the Great Lakes."

Craig Lake State Park

7hey improved the road to Craig Lake.
A logging company threw down some gravel and graded the forest road, and the staff at Van Riper State Park posted a few more directional signs. You no longer need a compass mounted to your dashboard to find the most remote state park in Michigan.

Too bad. There was no better way to begin an adventure into the state-designated wilderness than clutching the hand-drawn map they gave you at Van Riper, while bumping along seven miles of washed-out logging roads and gutted two-tracks. On my first trip, I got so lost going in that I never did find Craig Lake. On the second trip, I got lost coming out. My biggest fear each time has been that I would lose my muffler to the mud holes that reach the running boards of my partner's pick-up as it leads the way.

Pause, pray, and plunge in. But the effort is worth every rock ricocheting off your tailpipe.

When we finally reached the parking area and began portaging our gear in, when I finally stood on the shore of this 374-acre lake where eagles soar among the pines and moose wade along its shoreline, I felt miles from nowhere.

So did Frederick C. Miller, and that was precisely his intention. He wanted to lose himself in Michigan wilderness, and Craig Lake was his chosen destination.

Born in Milwaukee in 1906, Miller was the son of a prosperous family and owned, among other things, Miller Brewing Company. His first love was sports. For three years he was captain of his high school football team; in 1925 he enrolled at Notre Dame University, where he continued his gridiron career under the immortal Knute Rockne. Under Rockne's tutelage, Miller achieved his greatest success on the playing field, gaining All-American honors as a tackle and being named captain of the Fighting Irish as a senior.

After graduating *cum laude* from the university, Miller joined the brewery that was founded by his grandfather in 1855. Within 11 years, he was head of the corporation. Some time after he became president of the brewery, Miller's second love—of the outdoors and fishing—prompted him to begin looking for a wilderness retreat. By 1950 he had purchased Craig Lake and thousands of surrounding acres, including a dozen more lakes and the West Branch of the Peshekee River.

The first thing Miller did was to name many of the lakes. Craig and nearby Teddy were named for his sons; to the north, Clair Lake was christened in honor of his daughter; and to the northeast, High Life became perhaps the only lake in Michigan named after a beer.

Then Miller built his retreat. On a bay along the west side, he had a small, six-bunk cabin

LEFT: *A wood lily emerges from beneath a growth of evergreens.*

constructed for his caretaker and other hired help. On a point nearby, he specified a bunkhouse for large groups. And for himself and his family, he built Miller Lodge, sparing no expense despite the remote location. The lodge included huge, single-pane picture windows that overlooked the lake, hardwood floors, and a field stone fireplace in the main room that was a masterpiece of masonry. The fireplace was so large that it burned logs five feet long, and so ornate that metal busts of horses decorated the hearth.

The last thing Miller did was to place dams on the streams between the lakes, then stock the lakes with his favorite game fish. He planted bass in Crooked Lake, walleye in Craig, northern pike in Teddy, and muskie in Clair. He could rise in the morning and choose which fish he wanted to catch during the day, undisturbed on a lake all his own. A wilderness lover like myself can only dream of what that must have been like.

He had a spot cleared as a helicopter pad, but most of the time Miller, an accomplished pilot, would arrive in his float plane, taxiing right up to the lodge to spend a few quiet days in the splendor of Craig Lake, miles from nowhere. It was one man's personal wilderness, but it would not remain so for long.

Traveling in the corporate airplane, Miller and one of his sons died when the plane went down on December 17, 1954. The family quickly sold most of the land around Craig Lake to a logging company in Marquette, which in turn sold the Miller estate to the state of Michigan in the 1960s. In 1967, the Department of Natural Resources dedicated the wilderness tract as its newest state park. It's perhaps one of life's little ironies that I, a writer who will never amass fortune or prestige like Frederick Miller, have spent more time fishing his personal wilderness than he did.

But the family can keep the brewery. I'll take Craig Lake.

Year after year, I navigate the roads to lose myself in the lake's solitude, always returning convinced that there isn't another state park like it anywhere in Michigan. Or maybe in the Midwest. For starters, no park offers so much acreage, yet draws so few visitors.

Additional purchases by the state over the years have enlarged the park to almost 10,000 acres. Even though more and more people are "discovering" the remote wilderness, it's still rare for Craig Lake to be inhabited by more than a handful of parties at one time. "A busy weekend is 15 cars in the parking lot," said one ranger at Van Riper State Park, which administers Craig Lake. "It's rugged back in there."

Some of the most rugged trails in Michigan are back in there, and while they might slow up a few backpackers, what stops most people from entering the park is the logging road that takes you in, and the portage where the two-track ends. Even after you find the parking lot, Craig

Lake is a portage away. The trail is less than a half-mile long, but place a boat over your head and it seems more like two miles. A canoe is ideal for this park—especially a light one—for there are no boat launches on Craig Lake and motors are banned.

To reach the heart of the park, you either paddle or hike. A network of portages provides strong-shouldered paddlers with access to six lakes, while a nine-mile trail system permits backpackers to hike completely around Craig Lake. There are times on the trail when you emerge on the edge of a granite bluff to enjoy a spectacular panorama of the deep-blue lake and its rock-studded islets, or descend a ridge so steep that it leaves you wondering, "Is *this* Michigan?"

Backcountry camping is permitted anywhere in the park, as long as you set up at least 150 feet from the water. You can also stay at a pair of rustic campsites, one in Craig Lake's southeast corner and the other at the north end of Crooked Lake. Both provide fire rings and vault toilets.

But what may be the most unusual wilderness accommodation in Michigan is situated on the western shore of Craig Lake. The bunkhouse is long gone—struck by lightning and burnt to the ground—but for $25 a night, you can rent the caretaker's cabin. The small hut sleeps six; mattresses, a stove and refrigerator that run on LP gas, a rowboat with oars, and an outhouse up the hill are provided.

Or, better yet, live the life of a brewery magnate who loved the wilderness, even if it's only for a week. You can rent Miller Lodge, stone fireplace and all. Here you can relive Miller's cherished days in the woods, from the log chairs and tables where he sat to the backroom where he undoubtedly cleaned his fish at night. You can witness the same early-morning view of the water as the sun rises over a scattering of islands in the middle of Craig Lake.

ABOVE: A doe and her fawn
pause in a Michigan woods,
sensing an intruder.

RIGHT: Blueberries drenched in dew.
The wild berries begin ripening in late
July in the Upper Peninsula.

Despite its unusual history, most visitors who find their way to the park do so because of its fishing. At some point, a few of Miller's muskies found their way into Craig Lake, and today the lake is renowned for both muskie and pike. Special fishing regulations have been placed on the park that prohibit live bait and mandate that all muskie and pike must be returned, regardless of their size.

Other park visitors come simply to explore this wilderness. You can paddle east across Craig Lake, then portage a half-mile into Crooked Lake, well-named for its bays, inlets, and irregular shoreline. Head south, and you eventually arrive at a small channel that leads into two more lakes, the second reached only by pulling the canoe over a few beaver dams.

These lakes are unposted, unnamed, and usually undisturbed by other paddlers. If you do wander this far, you'll discover a large island in the middle of the second lake, an ideal place to set up camp and, at night, to watch for emerging wildlife. Deer will timidly come to the water's edge; beavers will swim past; eagles might be seen in the distance. If you're lucky, a portion of the Upper Peninsula's transplanted moose herd might even make an appearance.

You can wander anywhere in the park, with the exception of a small island in the middle of Clair Lake that contains a rustic log cabin. Here, miles from nowhere, you'll find an incongruous "No Tresspassing" sign. That's because the cabin and the island are yet owned by Clair Miller Krause, a piece of brewery trivia that's lost on most canoeists who paddle through Miller's own wilderness.

Above: A waxy yellow lady's slipper, also known as "moccasin flower." By either name, it's a pleasant sight for wildflower enthusiasts.

Right: An old boat protrudes above the mirrored surface of Trout Lake in Alger County. The lake is located on the west side of the county, south of Chatham.

Menominee River

My name is Right.

The man sitting behind me has the same name, but the woman across from me is named Left, as is everybody on that side of the raft.

The first thing you do when you're preparing to run the Piers Gorge of the Menominee River, Michigan's premier stretch of white water, is strap on a high flotation life jacket and helmet. The second thing you do is grab a paddle. And the last thing you do before shoving off into the granite gorge filled with holes, four-foot curls, and a ten-foot drop called Misicot, is give up your name.

"We change your name to the side of the boat you're on," said Mike Mehne of Argosy Rafting, a Wisconsin company that has been running the gorge for 16 years. "That gives people just two things to think about: Eat the waves, and if your name is called out, back paddle."

Never forget your name, even if you're about to hit the "Terminal Surfer," a hole big enough to sink a bus. Don't forget it even if the woman named Left is screaming her lungs out only inches from your ear.

"Right, right, right!" instructs Mehne.

All of us rafters named Right begin to back paddle furiously, partly because some of us remember the pre-float instructions, but mostly out of fear.

Then we're lost in a maddening sea, with huge waves slapping at us, rocks rushing past us, and a roar that sounds as if a 747 is taking off next to us. Forget your water slides and the log ride. You won't find anything at an amusement park as wild or as wet as what we're plunging into.

"It's an incredible river," says Mehne. "There's nothing like the power of a river, and the Menominee has as much power as anything you can raft commercially. It just doesn't have the length."

It's true. The Menominee is the merging of the Brule and Paint rivers northwest of Iron Mountain. From here, the longest river in the Upper Peninsula flows southeast, forming the border between two states before emptying into Lake Michigan between the towns of Menominee, Michigan, and Marinette, Wisconsin.

A border dispute between the two states led to the first official exploration of the river. Although native Americans and undoubtedly fur traders had traveled up the Menominee for years, the U.S. Congress commissioned Captain Thomas Jefferson Cram of the Army Corp of Engineers to survey the river in 1840, and to decide what was Wisconsin and what was Michigan.

Loggers followed in the 1880s, sending millions of trees down the Menominee to sawmills on the shores of Lake Michigan, where barges took the planks south to Chicago. The towering Upper Peninsula white pines were so big that it took only four logs to produce 1,000 board feet of lumber at the mills. They were so big that

LEFT: *Rafters begin the descent down Misicot Falls in the Menominee River's Piers Gorge.*

when the river rats driving timber down the Menominee reached the steep gorge south of Iron Mountain, they had trouble sending the pines through.

The Menominee's water was so wild and the current so strong that the timber would smash on boulders and along granite walls, or else would get so tangled up that dynamite was required to break up the log jams. To combat this, many locals say, lumbermen built a series of piers, or wooden chutes, to slow down the water and provide a safe path through the roar of the rapids.

By 1918 the loggers were gone, but the name stuck. Piers Gorge. The river was eventually harnessed for its power and dammed up, and for the most part it's now a wide and tranquil waterway.

Most of it. But not here in the gorge, where within a half-mile the Menominee descends 20 feet over rock ledges, past granite bluffs, and around boulders—one so large it's called Volkswagen Rock, because it looks like a Beetle parked in the middle of the current.

It's such wild water that this stretch has been the site of national kayaking competition, while serving as the bread-and-butter run for several rafting companies over the years. And that was the draw for us thrill-seekers immersing ourselves in white water for the first time. Forget the kayak. Don't even *think* about an inner tube.

Give up your name, and jump into a raft.

· · · · · · · ·

We began the day in Wisconsin, where guides issued the equipment and put us through a crash course in rafting.

Use both hands or no hands on the paddle. "Use one hand and you're guaranteed to lose some teeth," said one guide.

The worst place to be is on the floor of a raft, and if you fall out, put your hands on your life jacket and point your feet downstream. But above all else . . .

"Find the waves and eat them," said Mehne. "The way you stay inside the boat is by throwing yourself at the waves. The bigger the waves, the harder you throw yourself into them. Don't let them knock you down!"

Like a football team emerging for the second half, crews of six were led down the riverbank, and together we launched the 16-foot rafts. The

beginning was an easy float on flat water, but within 20 minutes we were swept into a short stretch of rapids known as Sand Portage Falls. The guides barked commands. No one forgot his name, and all six rafts bounced through the waves into tranquil conditions.

It was strictly a warm-up, and some paddlers were barely wet. "Hey, this is fun!" said a woman named Left. She joined the hooting, hollering, and high-fiving in our boat.

Brimming with newfound confidence, we floated a little longer, then pulled off to the side and followed Mehne up a steep bank to scout the gorge from a rocky knob 80 feet above the water. On the high point, we gathered around the head guide, peered down the steep sides, and gasped at an incredible display of roaring water. It was churning. It was swirling. It was curling. But most of all, it was dropping, for just upriver is Misicot Falls, a chute of smooth water that plummets 10 feet into a huge, curling wave five feet high. They call that smooth drop "the Tongue."

"There's the Tongue, Volkswagen Rock, Hell Hole, and it just keeps going on and on," said Mehne.

But *you* don't have to keep going. The reason for pulling up was to give people a chance to bail out. The Michigan side of the wild water is Piers Gorge Scenic Area where, at a parking area just off U.S. 8, a trail departs into the woods and skirts the rocky edge of the canyon. For almost a mile you can hike along and at every opening peer down into the gorge and watch the water tumble on its viscous course.

If you're a rafter and you suddenly find your heart in your throat and your knees knocking, you can just hike down the trail until you come to flat water again, and wait for the boats. Usually on these commercial runs, one or two people will be overwhelmed by the gorge and skip the rapids. "Except when somebody falls out on the first run—then there's usually a *lot* of people who skip it," said Mehne.

The veteran river runner loaded the first raft with ten of us. To compensate for the short stretch of white water, he packed the rafts with more people so he could offer everybody an opportunity to run this stretch twice. But no one

ABOVE: *The green darner, also called the "snake doctor," one of the fastest and biggest of the common dragonflies.*

OVERLEAF: *The moon appears while the sunset perfectly silhouettes a tree in Alger County.*

was thinking about the second run, because within minutes we would be where many of us never thought we would—on top of Misicot—and from the water it didn't look the way it did from 80 feet above.

It was even bigger. For a split second, we were on the edge of what rafters call "a horizontal drop," looking down the smooth Tongue at that huge standing wave at the bottom. Then we were rushing down. That's when the woman named Left began screaming into my ear.

"OOOhhh My Gawd!!!"

At the bottom we slammed into the wave, and the four of us in front, with arms locked, leapt forward and threw ourselves into a wall of water that was two feet higher than we were, even after we stood up. We ate a wave, in a goal-line defense that would have made Knute Rockne proud. But there was no time to celebrate.

"Left, left, left!" Mehne called out, and we managed to turn the raft just enough to avoid ricocheting off Volkswagen Rock. We shot through Hell Hole looking like experts.

But we weren't. Confusion reigned when some Rights didn't back paddle after their name was called out, and some Lefts didn't paddle at all. We approached Terminal Surfer, the last big hole, going backward. We flew through the drop like an out-of-control Tilt-A-Whirl and spun through the last of the heavy white water. When we finally hit the light rapids at the end of the Gorge, there was a bit of euphoria.

We had done it. We ate a wave and licked the Tongue. And 15 minutes after launching into the Gorge, or maybe only 10, we landed in a calm inlet, jumped out of the raft, and rushed up the trail to experience Michigan's wildest water all over again.

Every one of us, even the screamer named Left.

Tahquamenon Falls State Park

*B*uzzzzzzzz.

First there's the work. It ain't wild Michigan if you can drive through it on a four-lane paved highway, complete with rest stops and billboards directing you to the nearest motel.

That's why the pads of my portage yoke were digging into my shoulders. That's why I was crazy enough to put a canoe over my head and a pack on my back. That's why I was carrying all this baggage along a soft, sandy trail in Tahquamenon Falls State Park.

I'd seen the falls—practically driven right up to it and followed a paved path to a posted over-look. Now I wanted to see Betsy Lake, and I knew there had to be a way to reach it. You just had to work a little.

Buzzzzzzzz.

Then there was this deerfly buzzing around behind my head. I'd turn around quickly—as quickly as I could with a canoe over my head—and it would still be behind me. Clever little fly. I finally stopped, allowed it to land, then nailed it with a hard slap to the back of the neck with one hand while balancing the canoe with the other. I started up the trail with a fox's grin on my face, when suddenly I realized . . . there were now *two* flies pestering me from behind.

Buzzzzzzz.

Buzzzzzzz.

I ignored them and hustled up the trail, reaching Clark Lake after a 30-minute walk from the end of a rough two-track road. I threw my gear in the boat and paddled across the lake to its north side, slowly searching the shoreline for a portage trail I knew had to be there. It was. The trail was unmarked, but clearly visible among the pines.

Once again there was a portage yoke to slip on, a boat to be carried, a few flies to slap. The half-mile took 40 minutes to walk, as I banged trees along the way and grunted inside my fiber-glass shell. All I could see were the tips of my boots and a few feet of the trail in front of them. I had departed the visitors center at noon. When I finally reached my destination two-and-a-half hours later, it came as a surprise.

I heard the gentle sounds of lapping water, and when I lifted the canoe high above my head, there she was—Betsy Lake in all her splendor. The lake was very large, very beautiful, and all mine. I could see every inch of the two-mile-wide body of water, and there was not another soul on her. My shoulders ached; my neck was swollen with welts from the bites of deerflies; my ankles were tired from trudging through sand; but here was my reward. Here was a lake I could call my own, if only for an afternoon.

She was wild and priceless.

LEFT: A fallen maple leaf rests on the frosted leaves of blueberry bushes.

ABOVE: The Upper Falls at Tahquamenon Falls State Park. The cascade is the most impressive in Michigan, 200 feet across with a 48-foot descent into the Tahquamenon River.

The mighty Tahquamenon River rises from gurgling springs northwest of McMillan, and from a set of small lakes begins its long journey toward Lake Superior. It trickles along at first, then winds through a vast willow swamp where, in July, clouds of black flies have chased canoeists for miles down stream.

But the river grows with every stream that feeds it—Kings Creek, Syphon Creek, Red Creek, Silver Creek, on and on. At Newberry, the Tahquamenon has the volume and size of a major river, and when it reaches its final 16 miles within the state park, it's the heart and soul of what many call the U.P.'s "Superior Country." By the time its stained waters merge with the deep blue of Lake Superior, the Tahquamenon has drained an area of 900 square miles as it traveled 94 miles to Whitefish Bay.

The river is long. The park is big. At almost 40,000 acres, it's second in size only to the Porcupine Mountains within the state park system. But it's the falls that has always intrigued travelers passing through Superior Country, from the earliest Ojibwa Indians to contemporary families that motor through on their summer vacation.

The Upper Falls is the most impressive cascade in Michigan, and it's possibly the most beloved natural attraction in a state blessed with some of nature's finest handiwork. The falls is more than 200 feet across, with a 48-foot drop. It's often cited as the second-largest falls east of the Mississippi River in water volume, and the third-largest in terms of size. Only Niagara Falls in New York and Kentucky's Cumberland Falls have longer drops than the Tahquamenon's.

From the minute you step out of your car in the parking lot, you can hear the roar of the Upper Falls. After a half-mile walk you're standing on the edge of a steep gorge, staring at gallons of root beer—foam and all—spilling into a river of more. More than 50,000 gallons of the Tahquamenon flow over the Upper Falls every *second* when the river is high; a mere 2,000 gallons when it's not. Tannic acid from the cedar, hemlock, and willow swamps accounts for the root beer color of the water, which is extremely soft. When the water is churned by making the long drop at the falls, foam appears at the bottom and begins its journey east.

Four miles downstream is the Lower Falls. While it lacks the overwhelming power of its upstream counterpart, the Lower Falls has a charm all its own. The Lower Falls is a series of cascades with a total drop of 22 feet. In the middle of all these cascades lies a small island, and around the edge of the island is a foot trail. Step for step, this is one of the most beautiful footpaths in the state, but there's not a lot of steps. It's a loop of less than a mile that skirts the outside of the island, passing one display of tumbling water after another. On a summer day, hundreds come to the Lower Falls, rent a rowboat or canoe, and paddle over to the island. Here, they follow the trail and kick their shoes off at the first cascade they come to. They wade out to the submerged rock ledges and let the river cascade across their legs.

Ahhhhhhh! To many—especially to kids—the Upper Falls are more spectacular, but the Lower Falls are more fun.

Love of this falls and this river is not new. Indians, especially Ojibwa tribes, were attracted to the Tahquamenon, and they farmed, fished, and trapped along its banks. In the late 1800s the Tahquamenon was invaded by loggers who floated thousands of winter-cut trees to mills elsewhere. Many became the first permanent settlers of the area.

But two men in particular immortalized the Tahquamenon. The first was Henry Wadsworth Longfellow in his epic poem, "The Song of Hiawatha." The poet described the river as "the marsh of the blueberries," and had Hiawatha build his canoe "by the rushing Tahquamenaw."

The second man was outdoor writer Ben East who, with five companions, trekked 50 miles in 1929 from Soo Junction to the Upper Falls, through the winter wilderness of the Upper Peninsula. He wrote of three cold nights when the companions took turns sleeping and feeding the fire to keep it alive. He detailed the splendor of the U.P.'s winter, and recounted the excitement of finally reaching the falls. But what affected his readers the most and sparked a movement to preserve the river was his photos. East was the first to capture the frozen Upper Falls on film—a cascade held in place by the U.P.'s sub-zero winter.

The public was astounded, and began to clamor for a park. After elaborate negotiations and some major "horse trading" of other land, the state obtained 18,563 acres including the falls in 1947, turning it into Tahquamenon Falls State Park. The early settlers have long since been displaced by tourists—almost half a million make the pilgrimage to the falls every year. The vast majority come in the summer, pull into the parking area for a quick view of the Upper Falls, then zip on down the road to the next attraction.

They see but the smallest slice of the park. Beyond the falls and the campgrounds, the rest of the park is an undeveloped tract, free of roads, motels, and souvenir stands selling rubber tomahawks. The vast forest is broken only by a dozen lakes, ponds, and 25 miles of hiking trails.

Come in February. You can trudge through the deep snow and have any overlook to yourself, seeing the Upper Falls just as Ben East saw it. Slip on a pair of cross-country skis and stride through a stand of towering white pines along the Giant Pines Trail. Throw on a backpack and hike through the middle of the park along the North Country Trail, which reaches the shores of Lake Superior before departing south for the Mackinac Bridge.

Or bring your canoe and a portage yoke in August, and after fighting the crowds to see the falls, leave everyone behind and escape into the other half of the park. Carry your equipment into Clark Lake, paddle across, and portage to Betsy Lake. At the north end of Betsy, you'll find a long, narrow inlet and a small stream.

Squeeze your way down the stream, and you'll eventually emerge at Sheephead Lake. In this remote corner of the park, the roar of the Upper Falls is somewhere off in the distance, and all you can hear is the crazy laughter of a pair of loons.

Come here because some old-time Yooper once said he caught a 46-inch northern pike in Sheephead, and you aren't sure whether he was pulling your leg. Stay for the quiet.

RIGHT: A lesser golden plover in its winter plumage at Whitefish Point, north of Tahquamenon Falls State Park.

Sylvania Wilderness

He emerged from the early morning mist, sitting very straight but alone in a 17-foot canoe. He'd take a stroke with his paddle, then lay it across his lap while the boat glided through the mirror-like waters of Clark Lake, and when the craft was on the verge of losing its last bit of momentum, he'd casually take another.

He had just rounded a point into a long inlet when I spotted him from my campsite. He sat in the stern of the canoe rather than the middle, but had few problems controlling the front because the bow was laden with gear. His gear was as ancient as his red cedar canoe.

I had a geosphere dome tent made out of rip-stop nylon. He had a canvas lean-to that he waterproofed every spring and lashed together once he arrived at his campsite.

I had a backpacker's stove that roared from a bottle of white gas. He had a small iron grill.

I had a polyester-filled mummy bag. He had a set of blankets.

That night we both camped on the edge of Clark Lake in the Sylvania Wilderness. When I went down to the lakeshore to fill my water bottle, he nodded, held up a bottle of murky brown liquid, and said, "Need a nip to keep you warm?"

We both smiled, knowing that eventually liquor would chill our insides and send us

Left: Much of the impressive timber in the Sylvania Wilderness was spared from the logger's axe in the early 19th century.

scurrying in search of our bedding. But his fire had a friendly crackle to it, and the prospect of conversation was too inviting for me to pass up. I joined him for a tin cup that was battered and bruised and filled with exactly two fingers of good Kentucky whiskey. No ice, no frizzy soda, no cherry on a sword. Out here, those things aren't needed.

We nodded and sipped.

He was 68 years old, and he'd been coming to this area since long before it was designated wilderness—before it was even part of the Ottawa National Forest. There was a time when he was younger and his muscles stronger, a time when he would portage his canoe to the most remote lakes of the Sylvania tract. No easy task. His red cedar canoe exceeded 90 pounds. My Kevlar canoe was 35 pounds including the portage yoke.

But now he's grateful just to be around when June arrives, so he can pack his fly rods and a small cloth case of his favorite flies and ask somebody at the parking lot to help him carry his canoe to the edge of Clark Lake. Then he takes those long, smooth strokes until he rounds the point near the end of the lake to his favorite campsite.

"You fly-fish?" he asked. I nodded, but said I hadn't had much luck my first day, and he asked what I was using at the end of my line. I pulled a sponge beetle out of my pocket, and the eight rubber legs dangled in the warm glow of the fire.

"These are big bass in these waters," he said. "To catch big bass, you need big bait." He opened his case and passed one of his own over. It was obviously hand-tied, probably the week before. It was a streamer of sorts, with a deer hair collar dyed yellow, and long, flowing purple feathers tied in along the sides.

"I have a five-weight," I said. "My rod will never throw this."

"Mine will." He handed me a split cane rod and told me where to use it the next morning.

I was so stunned at his graciousness that I never asked why.

. . . .

This tract we call Sylvania is located in the western Upper Peninsula, adjacent to the Wisconsin-Michigan border at the south end of Gogebic County. Scattered throughout are 35 lakes, many of them connected by a series of por-

tages. It's no Boundary Waters, hardly comparable to the great million-acre canoe wilderness of northern Minnesota. Sylvania contains a mere 21,000 acres.

But it's special, and it's very wild—even for the Upper Peninsula. Glaciers were responsible for the area's topography, shaping its rolling hills and leaving the depressions that later became lakes and ponds. Through the 19th century and the first half of the 20th, much of Sylvania was spared the lumberman's axe, and many of its owners used the area as a personal retreat.

Thus the tract entered the 1960s with virgin stands of timber—trees that were more than 200 years old, including some that botanists believe date back to the 1500s. There are a few patches of white pine, and they easily tower above the treeline. But most of the forest is made up of northern hardwoods—sugar maple, yellow birch, hemlock, and basswood that, in mid to late September, turn brilliant shades of autumn colors.

Amidst the trees, the wildlife is abundant. Whitetail deer are plentiful; so are beavers, otters, fishers, porcupines, and many other small mammals. Campers are advised to string their food bags high in the trees, to bear-proof their camps from the black bears that roam the tract. Many visitors pack along a pair of binoculars and search the lakeshores for bald eagles, loons, ospreys, or a variety of waterfowl.

In 1966 Sylvania was purchased under the Land and Water Conservation Fund, becoming part of the Ottawa National Forest as the Sylvania Recreation Area. Rangers immediately put in a large-vehicle campground at the north end of Clark Lake, along with a picnic area and a developed beach. But the rest of the tract was so devoid of roads and so isolated that development was limited to small backcountry campsites scattered around the larger lakes. Each contained two or three tent pads, a fire ring, and a table. And that was it. Eighty-four of these sites were built at 29 different locations on eight of the larger lakes—and you couldn't drive to any of them. A few could be reached on foot, but most required a canoe and at least one portage.

The Forest Service also posted and mapped 30 miles of foot trails for those who wanted nothing to do with the water—paths that traversed the old-growth forests and passed the shores of many lakes. And finally, special fishing regulations were implemented to protect the trophy fish that had developed over the years due to the inaccessibility of the lakes. Only artificial lures were allowed—you couldn't use worms or other live bait to entice the fish. You couldn't fish before the last Saturday in April or after October, and you couldn't keep a bass, regardless of its size.

The rules and regulations were aimed at keeping a small but wild and pristine area wild and pristine. They worked. In late 1987, Sylvania was one of ten areas named in the Michigan Wilderness Act and added to the National Wilderness Preservation System. The Sylvania Wilderness is actually 18,327 acres, while the rest of the tract, which includes the developed campground and beach, has remained the "recreation area."

After the wilderness designation, the Forest Service eliminated some of the backcountry campsites to increase the solitude of the area, and began removing tables and fire rings. Small parties were encouraged and a permit system was implemented, so on a busy July weekend when all the backcountry campsites filled up, that was it. This area was too wild and pristine to be overrun, even by campers and canoers.

Now there's talk of a reservation system for the backcountry campsites, to ensure that if somebody drives ten hours to the Upper Peninsula with a canoe on top of his car, he'll have an opportunity to sample Sylvania. It's a modern-day dilemma. There are more wilderness lovers than there is wilderness, so a 21st-century solution is proposed: Come to Sylvania and reserve a slice of the wild for the weekend.

And they do. They come for the solitude; they come to hear the loons; but most of all they come for the lakes—the true gems of Sylvania. Of the tract's 21,000 acres, more than 4,000 are lakes, six of them larger than 250 acres.

What makes them so precious is their clarity. They sit on the divide between the Lake Superior and Mississippi River drainages, but have no surface outlet to either one. Nor do they have any rivers or streams pouring nutrient matter into them. They are 35 landlocked lakes fed by springs, bogs, and precipitation. They are, for all practical purposes, rain barrels with water so clear you can lean over the side of your canoe and see the bottom, 30 or 40 feet down.

. . . .

He'd directed me to a section of Clark Lake where a series of trees had been blown down along the shoreline. "The bass love that underwater forest," he said. They hung out among the branches, waiting for an unsuspecting minnow or a small bluegill to swim by.

"Run the fly along the trunk of each tree. Be careful not to get hung up on the protruding branches and you'll catch a bass," he said.

I followed his instructions. I'd cast and then strip in line, watching the purple feathers of the

ABOVE: *The moon rises over an inland lake. Sylvania Wilderness includes 35 lakes, six of which are larger than 250 acres.*

RIGHT: *Clark Lake is managed through special fishing regulations that protect the trophy bass that inhabit its waters.*

hand-tied fly flutter as if they were a lost minnow looking for the rest of the school. I'd twitch the tip of the rod, and the fly would dart and dive between the branches but wouldn't get hooked on the dead wood. The bamboo cane gave me that much control.

The clarity of the water amazed me. I saw everything—the fly, the branches, and finally, a dark oval shape that raced out from beneath the tree.

"Whoa!" I immediately raised the tip and yanked on the line with my free hand, and the wiggle of a head beneath the surface told me the hook was set. The bass tried to race back to the security of the submerged tree, but I horsed it toward the open water and, for the first time, wondered what pound tippet line he'd given me.

The bass changed its course and charged toward the canoe. I was stripping in line as fast as I could when it suddenly jumped. The entire fish came out of the water, and for a split second I could see the bronze stripes of a smallmouth bass reflect in the early morning sunlight.

A three-pound, four-pound, maybe five-pound bass? There was no time to speculate. The fish jumped a second and third time, then headed back to the shore. But the tippet held out and eventually won. The fish tired, and I carefully removed the hook from its upper lip.

I threw it back, of course. It's the law. But I would have released the bass anyway, even if I was allowed to keep it. It was his rod, his fly, his stretch of wilderness.

His fish.

ABOVE: A close look at the sort of rocky shoreline found in Negwegon State Park, along Lake Huron.

RIGHT: The steep, often slippery shoreline banks of Grand Sable Dunes in the Pictured Rocks National Lakeshore.

OVERLEAF: A golden sunrise over Lake Superior, near Grand Marais on the east end of the Pictured Rocks.